Developing Services for the Wireless Internet

Maurizio Morisio and Marco Torchiano (Eds)

Developing Services for the Wireless Internet

 Springer

Maurizio Morisio, PhD
Marco Torchiano, PhD
Politecnico di Torino, Italy

British Library Cataloguing in Publication Data
A catalogue record for this book is available from the British Library

ISBN-10: 1-4471-5698-6   Printed on acid-free paper
ISBN-13: 978-1-4471-5698-7

9 8 7 6 5 4 3 2 1

Springer Science+Business Media
springer.com

Contributors

Fabio Bella
Fraunhofer IESE
Fraunhofer-Platz 1
67663 Kaiserslautern, Germany
fabio.bella@fraunhofer.iese.de

Filippo Forchino
Motorola GSG Italy
Via Cardinal Massaia 92
10100 Torino, Italy
filippo.forchino@motorola.com

Tuomas Ihme
VTT Technical Research
  Centre of Finland
Kaitoväylä 1,
P.O. Box 1100, FIN-90571 Oulu,
  Finland
tuomas.ihme@vtt.fi

Jarmo Kalaoja
VTT Technical Research
  Centre of Finland
Kaitoväylä 1,
P.O. Box 1100, FIN-90571 Oulu,
  Finland
jarmo.kalaoja@vtt.fi

Paivi Kallio
VTT Technical Research
  Centre of Finland
Kaitoväylä 1,

P.O. Box 1100, FIN-90571 Oulu,
  Finland
paivi.kallio@vtt.fi

Heimo Laamanen
TeliaSonera
Teollisuuskatu 13
FIN-00051, Helsinki, Finland.
heimo.laamanen@teliasonera.com

Patricia Lago
Vrije Universiteit
De Boelelaan 1081a
1081 HV Amsterdam, The Netherlands
patricia@cs.vu.nl

Maurizio Morisio
Politecnico di Torino
Corso Duca degli Abruzzi 24
10129 Torino, Italy
maurizio.morisio@polito.it

Jürgen Münch
Fraunhofer IESE
Fraunhofer-Platz 1
67663 Kaiserslautern, Germany
juergen.muench @fraunhofer.iese.de

Mario Negro Ponzi
Motorola GSG Italy
Via Cardinal Massaia 92
10100 Torino, Italy
mario.negroponzi@motorola.com

Eila Niemela
VTT Technical Research
  Centre of Finland
Kaitoväylä 1,
P.O. Box 1100, FIN-90571 Oulu,
  Finland
eila.niemela@vtt.fi

Alexis Ocampo
Fraunhofer IESE
Fraunhofer-Platz 1
67663 Kaiserslautern, Germany
alexis.ocampo@fraunhofer.iese.de

Aki Tikkala
VTT Technical Research
  Centre of Finland

Kaitoväylä 1,
P.O. Box 1100, FIN-90571 Oulu,
  Finland
aki.tikkala@vtt.fi

Marco Torchiano
Politecnico di Torino
Corso Duca degli Abruzzi 24
10129 Torino, Italy
marco.torchiano@polito.it

Bruno Zanzottera
Investnet Italia SPA
Via Federico Confalonieri, 29
20124 Milano, Italy
b.zanzottera@investbv.com

Contents

1. Introduction **1**
Maurizio Morisio, Marco Torchiano

  1.1 What is peculiar to wireless services
      development? 1
  1.2 The WISE project 3
  1.3 Overview of chapters and reading guide 4

2. Software Development Processes **9**
Alexis Ocampo, Fabio Bella, Jürgen Münch

  2.1 The reference process model 9
  2.2 Requirements 12
  2.3 Design 15
  2.4 Coding 19
  2.5 Plan Testing 22
  2.6 Testing 24
  2.7 Life Cycle Process Models 27
  2.8 Conclusions 28

3. Technology **33**
Mario Negro Ponzi, Heimo Laamanen

  3.1 The Environment 33
  3.2 Wireless Networks Overview 35
  3.3 Hardware 39
  3.4 Programming Technologies (Languages and
      Frameworks) 44
  3.5 Cross Development 67
  3.6 To Sum Up 67

4. Software Architecture of Wireless Services.............................. **70**
Jarmo Kaloja, Tuomas Ihme, Patricia Lago, Eila Niemela,
Marco Torchiano

   4.1 Introduction 70
   4.2 Notation.. 71
   4.3 A reference architecture of wireless services 76
   4.4 Building typical wireless architectures with patterns.................. 85
   4.5 Conclusion.. 97

5. WISE Experience Pearls **100**
Fabio Bella, Tuomas Ihme, Jarmo Kalaoja, Paivi Kallio,
Mario Negro Ponzi, Alexis Ocampo, Aki Tikkala, Marco Torchiano

   5.1 Documentation format of a pearl.. 100
   5.2 The pearl system... 101
   5.3 Catalogue... 103

6. Pilot Projects **131**
Fabio Bella, Filippo Forchino, Jarmo Kalaoja, Jürgen Münch,
Alexis Ocampo, Mario Negro Ponzi, Marco Torchiano

   6.1 Pilot 1... 132
   6.2 Pilot 2... 140
   6.3 Conclusion.. 154

7. Glossary.. **157**
   7.1 Terminology.. 157
   7.2 Acronyms... 157

Index **161**

1
Introduction

MAURIZIO MORISIO, MARCO TORCHIANO

The wireless Internet is fast becoming a reality. Accessing the Internet and Internet protocol-based services through mobile wireless devices is already a reality for some and is just around the corner for most other people. The necessary infrastructure consisting of mobile terminals on one side and large bandwidth digital networks on the other is now available.

Given the penetration of cellular phones (roughly one device per active person in an ever increasing number of countries), the impact potential of the wireless Internet on both business and consumer applications is huge.

However, the availability of digital networks and terminals is not enough. The success of the wireless Internet has to be fuelled by the availability of wireless-specific services and applications. Otherwise, its business potential will not be fully exploited and voice based services will remain prevalent.

The development of wireless data services is a problem from a non-technical point of view, new business and billing models are required as well as new ideas for services. From a technical point of view, specific challenging issues arise because techniques and methods traditionally used for wireline Internet services may or may not work in a wireless context.

This book addresses mainly the technical issues, providing methods and techniques to support teams that develop wireless services.

The remainder of this chapter first describes what is unique about the development of wireless services, then briefly summarises the wireless Internet service engineering (WISE) project that produced the results presented in this book and finally provides a readers' guide for the book.

1.1 What is Peculiar to Wireless Services Development?

Techniques and methods traditionally used to develop wireline services and applications cannot be just transplanted into the wireless services world because new problems and constraints apply. This section describes the peculiarities of wireless services and how they influence the development of services.

Mobile Terminals. Mobile terminals, despite the tremendous improvements seen in the last few years are and will probably remain, more limited than PCs and other fixed terminals. The user interface is more limited; screens are smaller, input devices are reduced (keyboard with few keys, no mouse, and limited trackball).

In addition, processing power and memory storage must be reduced compared with fixed equipment due to size and power constraints.

Bandwidth and Quality of Service. Mobile networks usually offer more limited bandwidth and quality of service (QoS) than wireline networks. In a mobile network the radio environment can change very rapidly, causing both bandwidth and quality of service to change very rapidly with less predictably and with wider variation than in their wireline counterpart.

Mobile Interaction. Mobile users have a different interaction style with the terminal and the service than wireline users. This is partly due to the differences in the terminal indicated above and partly due to user approach; a mobile user has less time and is more easily distracted than a wireline user. As a result the interaction period of a mobile user is short and the user may approach the mobile device with a different attitude than when approaching a fixed line device. A mobile service must also consider the usability issue from a new point of view which could be called mobile usability.

Variability of Terminals. Mobile terminals come in a larger variety than fixed terminals in terms of wireless technologies supported and therefore bandwidth and QoS, input and output devices (keyboard, size and resolution of screen, etc.), processing and memory capability, operating systems and platforms. Ideally, a service should be capable of running on any terminal. In practice a service developer must often choose to support a subset of terminals.

Change of Technology. Due to the rapid change in underlying technology, a terminal is obsolete in two to three years at most. This poses another constraint on service developers since services will become obsolete in the same amount of time or less. From a business point of view, the return on investment (ROI) has to be obtained in a very limited time span. From a project management point of view, services must be developed and deployed in terms of months and should be isolated as much as possible from technological changes.

Unstable Business Models, Billing Models. As is common in newly emerging domains, no clear and stable business models exist nor do the related billing models (charging for time, for amount of data exchanged, for QoS, for type of service, for content, etc.). Service operators are still trying new models or refining existing ones. This phenomenon was also seen in the wired Internet domain. As a result, requirements for a service can change very quickly, both on the functional side and on the supporting side, such as billing, accounting and so on.

Incomplete Testing Environment. The variability (in networks, in terminals, in technology) implies that building a realistic environment for testing either the service or the business model is rarely feasible in terms of time and resources needed.

In summary, the domain of wireless services is extremely challenging since solutions must satisfy difficult and conflicting requirements including:

- Robustness in the face of variation of bandwidth and QoS, seamless change of network (e.g. from GSM to UMTS)
- Usability with diverse and reduced input/output devices
- Interaction style suitable for a mobile user
- Independence from the variability of terminals
- Independence from the evolution of technology
- Short development and deployment cycles
- Volatility of requirements
- Difficulty in building a realistic testing environment

This book provides techniques and methods to address these problems, building on the conceptual toolset developed in software engineering and other disciplines but also adapting it to the wireless domain.

The key concepts used can be summarised under three headings:

- Software process. Flexible, iterative and incremental processes are the starting point to support the high variability in requirements and short development cycles. Based on these concepts, Chapter 2 describes a reference process.
- Technology. The impact of different technologies is so important that a developer must be aware of them and of their overall effect, if not of all the detailed impact. An overview of current technologies is provided in Chapter 3.
- Architecture. A service developer usually does not have time to develop a service from scratch but will have to reuse existing building blocks, combining them in new and meaningful ways. A reference architecture and a taxonomy of lower level services to drive the composition effort are given in Chapter 4.

1.2 The WISE Project

This book is the result of the WISE project (http://softeng.polito.it/projects/WISE). WISE (wireless Internet service engineering) was funded by the European Commission under the IST (information society technologies) Research Programme, contract number IST-2001-30028.

The following partners carried out the project from 2001 to 2004.

The goal of the project was to develop methods and techniques to support the development of wireless services. This book contains the key results of the project.

The project was not just theoretical but has applied its preaching: techniques and methods developed in the initial phase of the project were then applied to implement two pilot projects: a service for mobile online trading and a mobile multiplayer game. The pilots are presented in Chapter 6.

As this was a collaborative project, each chapter description here identifies the partners and individuals responsible for each chapter.

Politecnico di Torino (Italy), a technical university and the project coordinator,
http://www.polito.it
http://softeng.polito.it

Fraunhofer IESE (Germany), a centre for applied experimental software engineering
http://www.iese.fraunhofer.de

Investnet (Italy), a provider of Internet based stock trading systems and services
http://www.investbv.com

Motorola GSG (Italy), the software division of Motorola
http://www.motorola.it

Solid EMEA North (Finland), a provider of data replication and synchronisation products
http://www.solidtech.com

TeliaSonera (Finland), a network operator
http://www.teliasonera.com

VTT Technical Research Centre of Finland (Finland), a research centre http://www.vtt.fi

1.3 Overview of Chapters and Reading Guide

The structure of the book mirrors the key issues in wireless Internet service development:

- Defining a suitable software development process (Chapter 2).
- Understanding technological constraints and making key technical decisions (Chapter 3).
- Defining suitable software architecture to support the service (Chapter 4). Despite the variations in the architecture, small isolated stand-alone solutions are provided for recurring problems. These are described as 'pearls' (Chapter 5).
- Learning from practice (Chapter 6). The concepts and techniques of earlier chapters are applied to two industrial projects.

This introduction was authored by Maurizio Morisio and Marco Torchiano of the Politecnico di Torino. Emails {Maurizio.Morisio, Marco.Torchiano}@polito.it

Chapter 2, Software Development Processes

Using the right technology and defining an effective architecture are the two key factors in developing a successful wireless Internet service. However, they are insufficient if not embedded in an effective development process. This chapter supports the reader in defining an effective process, the third factor of a successful project.

There is relatively little expertise of the characteristics of wireless service development, resulting in inadequate knowledge of development procedures and technical constraints for such services. The result is insufficient guidance for project managers and software developers on selecting appropriate development processes, techniques, methods and tools. The end result is poor quality products, unmotivated developers and managers and, eventually, unhappy users.

At the moment, there is very little experience in developing software for such services systematically. Therefore, designing processes for this domain entails several difficulties.

1. Whereas several tried and trusted methods exist for conventional software production which have been developed over many years, no such standard methods are available for wireless Internet services and existing methods do not translate directly into the mobile world.
2. The domain of wireless Internet service development lacks specific experience of particular technologies, their applicability and constraints, mainly due to the novelty and rapid rate of evolution of the technologies
3. The variations of the applications and, as a consequence, possible variations of the development technologies are poorly understood.

This chapter describes an initial reference process by summarising essential characteristics of the development of wireless Internet services and the impact of these technologies on life cycle, engineering and managerial process levels. The reference process is based on a comprehensive literature survey and experience from the pilot projects described later in the book. The reader is intended to be able to start a project using the reference process and customising it where required.

This chapter was authored by Alexis Ocampo, Fabio Bella, Jürgen Münch of the Fraunhofer IESE. Emails are {Alexis.Ocampo, Fabio.Bella, Juergen.Muench} @fraunhofer.iese.de

Chapter 3, Technology

The technological context always plays a key role in defining a product and this is especially true in the wireless area, where technology evolves at a swift pace. The aim of this chapter is to make the reader aware of what the relevant technologies are (mostly in the software sense, such as J2ME, BREW, html, WML, etc.) and to quantify their impact on the wireless service.

The major benefit of this chapter is not merely in listing a set of technologies that will certainly significantly evolve and change over the next few years, but in offering a framework to evaluate the effect of these technologies on the end product and, significantly, on its software architecture.

The framework characterises mobile devices from the physical level (such as processing and memory capacity, screen size, etc.) up to logical levels (fat vs. thin clients, rich vs. poor interaction).

The reader will become aware of these choices, of their pros and cons and of possible tradeoffs.

In the next chapter, requirements for the software architecture are derived from these choices.

This chapter was authored by Mario Negro Ponzi of Motorola GSG in Italy and Heimo Laamanen of Telia Sonera. Emails are Mario.Negroponzi@motorola.com and Heimo.Laamanen@teliasonera.com

Chapter 4, Software Architectures of Wireless Services

The software architecture of an application or service is a key resource in satisfying the requirements, exploiting the underlying technology as much as possible, making it possible to evolve the requirements over time and surviving technological changes.

This chapter provides guidance to develop sound software architecture for a wireless service. The chapter is organised in three parts:

- Introduction of a UML based notation extended to support wireless concepts. The notation is then used in the next two parts
- Presentation of a reference wireless architecture
- Presentation of some typical design patterns

The reader uses the reference architecture as a conceptual framework that defines basic concepts and terminology, the main components and their relationships. It is a high-level starting point to define the architecture for any specific application. The reader defines the necessary architecture by example starting from the reference architecture.

This chapter was authored by Jarmo Kaloja, Eila Niemela and Tuomas Ihme of VTT Electronics and Patricia Lago, and Marco Torchiano of the Politecnico di Torino. Patricia Lago is now with Vrije Universiteit Amsterdam.

Emails are {Jarmo.Kaloja, Tuomas.Ihme, Eila.Niemela}@vtt.fi; P.Lago@cs. vu.nl and Marco.Torchiano@polito.it

Chapter 5, WISE Experience Pearls

Typical architectures represent high-level solutions to problem situations. However, when examining problems in detail, there seem to be a set of fine-grained solutions to situations that occur frequently. This is the well-known idea of design patterns that has been adapted to this methodology. Here, they are called pearls and apply to a series of different stages of problem decomposition:

- architectural patterns
- design patterns

- technological solutions
- lessons learned

In this chapter a number of pearls that can be used in wireless architectures are described using a common documentation structure.

This chapter has a reference style, and does not require sequential reading. Each pearl is defined in terms of its:

- Context
- Problem
- Solution
- Design rationale

The reader uses the pearls by example, applying them as necessary to an individual project when the contexts of the pearl and the project match.

This chapter was authored by Fabio Bella and Alexis Ocampo of Fraunhofer IESE, Tuomas Ihme, Paivi Kallio, Aki Tikkala and Jarmo Kalaoja of VTT Electronics, Mario Negroponzi of Motorola GSG and Marco Torchiano of Politecnico di Torino

Emails are {fabio.bella, alexis.ocampo}@iese.fraunhofer.de; {Tuomas.Ihme, Jarmo.Kalaoja, Paivi.Kallio, Aki.Tikkala}@vtt.fi; Mario.Negroponzi@motorola. com and Marco.Torchiano@polito.it

Chapter 6, Sample Projects

During the WISE project two industrial level wireless services were developed; an online trading system and a multiplayer interactive role game. The experience from these projects is the foundation of all the material presented in the previous chapters.

This chapter briefly presents the case studies and how the guidelines presented in the previous chapters were applied in their development. For each project the process used, the technology, the architecture and a baseline of process measures are described.

The sample projects are presented as a comprehensive example of how all the techniques and methods presented in the book fit together.

This final chapter was authored by Fabio Bella of Fraunhofer IESE, Filippo Forchino of Motorola GSG Italy, Jarmo Kalaoja of VTT Electronics, Jürgen Münch and Alexis Ocampo of Fraunhofer IESE, Mario Negro Ponzi of Motorola GSG Italy, Marco Torchiano of Politecnico di Torino.

Emails are {Fabio.Bella, Alexis.Ocampo, Juergen.Muench}@fraunhofer.iese. de; {Filippo.Forchino, Mario.Negroponzi}@motorola.com; Jarmo.Kalaoja@vtt.fi and Marco.Torchiano @polito.it

1.3.1 Reading Paths

This book is intended to satisfy the needs of different categories of readers with different goals such as project managers, software architects and developers. Each

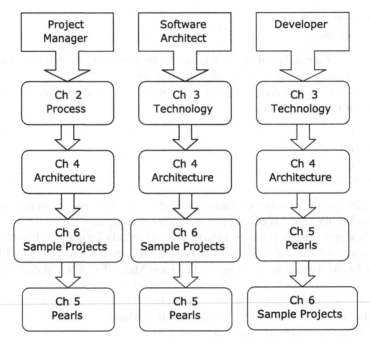

FIGURE 1.1. Reading paths for different reader categories.

one may find it advantageous to follow a slightly different reading path through the book, as shown in Figure 1.1.

A project manager should start with Chapter 2 to gain a complete picture of all the issues in a wireless project, continue with a skimming of Chapters 3 and 4, before studying Chapter 6 with special reference to the project management metrics. Finally the project manager will browse through the pearls to select the ones most relevant.

A software architect would browse through the process chapter before reading Chapters 3, 4 and 6 carefully, finally browsing Chapter 5, concentrating on design pearls.

A developer should follow a path similar to the one of a software architect. However, there should perhaps be more focus on the pearls and less on the architectural part.

2
Software Development Processes

ALEXIS OCAMPO, FABIO BELLA, JÜRGEN MÜNCH

The complexity and newness of the technology set that can be used for developing wireless Internet services (i.e. mobile terminals, mobile networks, mobile interaction, variety of terminals) and extreme time-to-market pressure result in insufficient knowledge about development procedures and technical constraints. The effect of this is inadequate guidance for project managers and software developers when selecting appropriate development processes, techniques, methods and tools. The end result is poor quality of products, unmotivated developers and managers and unhappy users.

Currently, there is very little experience in systematically developing software for such services. There are several reasons why difficulties are met in the design processes for this domain:

1. Whereas several standards exist for conventional software development such as IEEE 1074-1997, ISO 12207, CMM and CMMI, no such standards are available for wireless Internet services.
2. Due to its newness, the wireless Internet services domain lacks specific experience on particular technologies, their applicability and constraints.
3. The variations of the applications and variations of the development technologies, are poorly understood.

This chapter describes an initial reference process by summarising guidelines and providing several hints to account for the development of wireless Internet services at the levels of engineering processes and life cycle processes. The reference process is based on experience from the WISE pilot projects (see Chapter 6) and a comprehensive literature survey.

2.1 The Reference Process Model

The lack of knowledge on the part of software developers of the capabilities and characteristics of different wireless technologies, the expected major growth of this type of application in future years and the need for a systematic approach for developing these applications justify the creation of a reference process. This process has been derived and validated by means of the development of pilot projects and literature study [49].

The term 'software process reference model' is used to refer to a model that integrates consistent and validated empirical and theoretical evidence of processes, products, roles and tools used for developing software in a domain.

Creating a reference process solely by observing software projects is limiting in the level of detail and precision and may vary according to the particular project organisations in which the projects were executed. To counter this, the developed reference process was enhanced selectively with input from other sources such as the literature and experience reports from similar projects.

2.1.1 Notation

Table 2.1 shows the original entities used by the SPEARMINT® notation [48] with the addition of two new symbols which are required to understand the reference process model descriptions.

The SPEARMINT® notation uses the following entities:

- Artifacts
- Activities
- Role
- Tools

The last two rows in Table 2.1 present the symbols that are used for grouping those sets of activities that are considered optional or alternative in the reference process model.

TABLE 2.1. Entities and icons

Entity	Icon
Artifact	
Activity	
Roles	
Tools	
Alternative Box	ALT
Optional Box	OPT

TABLE 2.2. Relationships and icons

Relationship	Icon
The activity consumes the artifact	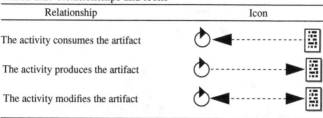
The activity produces the artifact	
The activity modifies the artifact	

The flow between artifacts is depicted by product flow graphs which contain activities, artifacts and the relationships between them (see Table 2.2).

2.1.2 Reference Process Model Overview

The above reference process model is a composite of the original process descriptions used in the WISE pilots (see Figure 2.1). Examining Figure 2.1, it appears rather like a waterfall development model but in practice it was followed by the pilots in a manner nearer to an incremental model. In this figure, activities are grouped into phases. This is because this figure reflects the highest level of abstraction of the model. Each phase will be expanded in the remainder of this chapter.

In order to understand the meaning of the two optional boxes in Figure 2.1, it is relevant to take a brief look at the process models actually followed by each pilot (for more details, see Chapter 6).

The life cycle model followed by pilot 1 was an iterative process model consisting of three phases: a requirements phase, a coding phase and a testing phase. One important characteristic of this development process was the absence of an explicit design phase. This was a direct consequence of reusing the same client–server architecture previously used to provide the same service on the traditional wired Internet. The pilot development went through three iterations. In all of them, design as such was not explicitly performed and thus the application prototype and its high level design were documented after development.

In pilot 2, different teams in different organisations were responsible for the development of the client on the mobile device and the multimedia layer on the server side. Both organisations followed an iterative life cycle model consisting of four phases: requirements, design, coding and testing phases.

The reference process model was reviewed and approved by software developers within their respective organisations. The final agreement among developers was to consider the design phase optional. However, pilot 1 developers decided to establish this phase as an option for future projects. Optional in this case means an activity that can be skipped by software organisations; for example when the service is being based on a known service such as an existing wired one. The same applied to the plan testing phase.

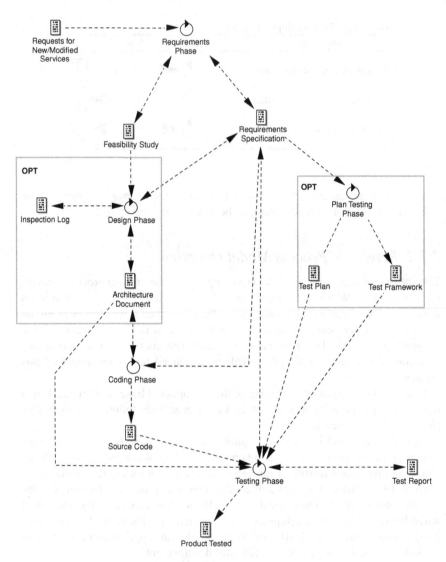

FIGURE 2.1. Reference process model.

2.2 Requirements

2.2.1 Guidelines Based on Experience

The purpose of the requirements phase is to produce clear and unambiguous requirements. This is subdivided into: select requirements, feasibility study and requirements specification.

In the WISE project pilots, the requirements were itemised in meetings with the customer. The marketing group informally communicated usability requirements

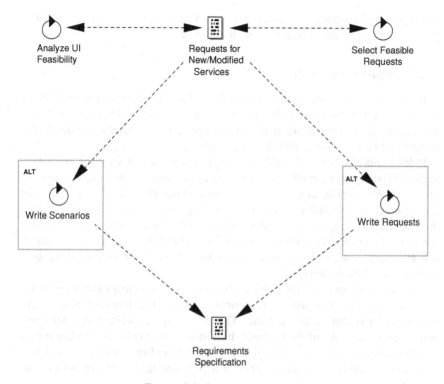

FIGURE 2.2. Select requirements.

to developers. Informal meetings were held between developers and marketing personnel and based on existing knowledge, discussions about best probable usability experience were held.

Open questions usually triggered a feasibility study, in which prototypes were developed to investigate current technologies (i.e., devices and networks) and understand its real capability. The interaction between customer and developer as well as the feasibility studies were considered to be of great value by pilot developers and therefore have been included as pearls in Chapter 6 of this book, identified as: 'Customer Requirement gathering' and 'Feasibility Study'.

Figure 2.2 shows two alternative boxes. This reflects the fact that although both projects produced a document with the application's requirements, the modus operandi was different.

Pilot 2 documented at a high level the functions of the service by using UML use cases that refined the client and server functional requirements. Additionally, performance and usability requirements were specified as part of the non-functional requirements. Pilot 1 did not use a special format for documenting the services' functionality. Both options were considered valid and therefore included in the reference process model by developers (write scenarios (UML), write requests).

A template and an example were agreed on and produced as part of the reference process and can be found at http://wise.iese.fhg.de.

2.2.2 Input from Other Work

A number of techniques used in related fields such as Internet or wireless software development were considered relevant and are included here as additional assistance for software developers and managers. The same also applies to the remaining phases of the reference process model.

Index Cards [16] are proposed by the usage-centred design approach as a mechanism to specify requirements as part of an agile usage-centred engineering approach for Web applications. Here customers, managers and developers collect the requirements on cards during a brainstorming session. The participants sketch the application's purpose from a business point of view and express their wishes regarding functionality, features, content and capabilities. The cards are sorted and clustered. The resulting clusters are taken as the basis for specifying user requirements functionality.

Extreme programming [15] proposes 'user stories' as a means to capture functional requirements in a simple, non-formal language. The developer writes them with the collaboration of the customer. The user stories are written on index cards and describe the tasks of the system. These stories are the basis for planning iterations, tracking progress, specifying and testing the functionality. User stories seem to be suitable for requirements that appear late in the development of the application.

The index cards and user stories involve customers under the assumption that they are participative and proactive and that they actually represent the user's needs. This might not be true in all cases. A review of the requirements by experts could compensate for this problem.

In order to address usability, the user-centered approach [17] assigns the business group of a software organisation to the tasks of studying and defining the profiles of its possible users. The profiles are used to determine possible tasks and goals of the users, specifying the functional requirements and creating a prototype for user analysis. The prototype consists of user interfaces that will be discussed with potential users and then implemented taking into account the feedback. In a heterogeneous market like wireless Internet services, this approach is seen as valuable because it forces development organisations to consider a wider spectrum of possible profiles.

Combinations of the above approaches could be applied depending on the context of the software development organisation. For instance, a large software development organisation has more resources for looking at the requirements than a small organisation up to a whole marketing department and director.

Regarding device independence, a good starting point for clarifying the concepts is given by a survey that presents a classification of available technologies and their relationship to device independence in the context of wireless Internet services [2]. For example, device attributes like output, input, processor, memory, multimedia objects, application language or browser language influence the degree of independence of an application. Devices receive content as multimedia objects, application languages or browser content. Depending on the underlying hardware, devices are able to use different types of content. Therefore, in order to achieve device independence, the content must be sent in formats compatible with all devices to be supported.

There are technologies that can be used to adapt the content or application according to the device capabilities. Content adaptation can be done in the server, proxy or client browser. Some examples of these technologies are: HTTP request header files, CC/PP composite capability preference profile, WAP UAPROF, SyncML and Universal plug and play.

This survey [2] is a good reference for understanding how each of the above mentioned technologies can help when trying to deliver a device-independent application. The bad news is that at the moment, there is no dominant or unique standard and therefore choosing a specific technology can imply high risks.

In order to mitigate this risk, the W3C consortium is working on an initiative focusing on device independence and standardisation. The idea is that web content and applications are accessible anyhow and anytime. Anytime refers to many access mechanisms described as heterogeneous clients that can provide access anytime, and anyhow refers to many modes of use including audio, voice and touch. One product of this effort is the device independence principles document [18]. At the moment, the principles are general, but they will be refined with guidelines and requirements to obtain device independence as well as to concentrate all standardisation efforts in one place.

2.3 Design

2.3.1 Guidelines Based on Experience

The purpose of this phase is to produce high- and low-level designs that meet the requirements specification. Figure 2.3 shows the high-level design, low-level design and design inspection activities. Briefly, each level of design can be represented by four viewpoints: structural, behavioural, deployment and development. The WISA (wireless Internet service architecture) architectural guidelines introduced in Chapter 4 are used as input for preparing the architecture document.

1. The architectural guidelines are made up of a set of viewpoints to model the conceptual/concrete architecture. Each viewpoint describes a particular architectural aspect;
2. There is a notation (languages and/or visual conventions) selected for the model and representing each viewpoint. The views and diagrams in the architecture document must be based on these viewpoints and conform to the notation.

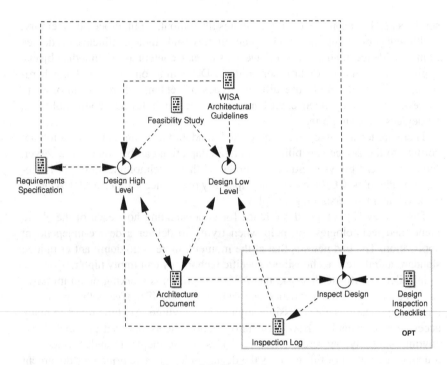

FIGURE 2.3. Design phase.

The structural viewpoint covers the composition of information and architectural components, whereas the behavioural viewpoint considers the dynamic aspects of the architecture. The deployment viewpoint shows the allocation of architectural components to physical nodes of computing and network environments. The development viewpoint maps the organisation and the choice of technologies to services and components. More details on the viewpoints, the notation and guidelines on how to describe them are provided in Chapter 4.

The design should be inspected based on a checklist and an established procedure. This activity is marked as optional, because it could be skipped once the organization's expertise and knowledge of the domain are mature enough.

Pilot developers recommend designing an user interface that avoids graphical controls that can only be used by a mouse device or touch screen. In other words, when designing the application, keep in mind that it also has to be suitable for the most limited devices. Developers consider this practice of great importance in order to avoid the cost of producing the same application several times for different devices. More references on designing for device independence are provided in the next section. Additionally, a pearl on 'device independence', can be found in Chapter 6 of this book.

Regarding technical features like scalability, quality of service (QoS) and billing models, the creation of components or agents responsible for such issues is recommended. One example is the service management component created in the WISE project, which provides services for authentication, authorisation, user profile management, provisioning and billing. Another example is an agent that negotiates the preferences of a client to accommodate the limitations of the server to provide the service. Network bandwidth limitations can be addressed by trying to optimise the data exchange rate and to reduce the amount of data sent over the network to the minimum. More examples of possible components can be found in the taxonomy of services provided in Chapter 4.

2.3.2 Input from Other Work

A survey performed across 25 organisations in the UK [6] revealed that formalised design web techniques such as hierarchy charts, site flow charts and storyboards were used in the web domain. Hierarchy charts were used to relate web pages of one site. Site flow charts sketched the decisions to achieve a certain functionality and storyboards contain the sequence of web pages that a user will encounter within a web site. These techniques were used to design the navigation of the structure.

Some of the companies studied had developed website layout standards for using video, animation, graphics, colours and navigational standards such as, where to place the back button and the use of banners and menus. Standards for designing website content were also found for example, in the use of specific keywords.

Examples of the use of structured techniques are given by references [1], [4], [19] and [20]. Their common feature is the use of object-oriented principles to design static and dynamic views of a wireless Internet service application. Patterns like the MODEL-VIEW-CONTROLLER are recommended for use in wireless Internet service applications by Kovari et al. [1], where the logic is concentrated on the server and a minimum or none of the business logic is revealed on the client side.

The use of this pattern can have additional benefits in that all the components are defined logically so that each component has a function, interfaces are defined between components, each component can be implemented as another pattern, high reusability, high flexibility resulting in reduced cost and higher quality. For more details on this pattern see Chapter 4.

Regarding device independence, Giannetti [21] describes the device independence web application framework (DIWAF). This framework is based on the 'single authoring' principle consisting of designing for the most capable device and automatically adapting content to different device classes. Content, layout and style are separated for reuse whenever possible.

Scalableweb is a technique presented in [22] that allows authors to build a device-independent presentation model at design time. Scalableweb is also based on the single authoring technique, where authors can produce the layout specification for the largest screen size of a given device and then a rendering system renders the device presentation model into device-specific presentations [27].

Mori et al. [23] present an XML-based approach oriented towards design applications that are device independent. One common feature between scalableweb and the XML-based approach is the specification of a task model as input for creating the device presentation model or the abstract user interface, which are later transformed into the device specifics with the help of an automatic or semiautomatic tool.

A high-level description of content, style and interaction that allows adaptation is important in order to achieve device independence.

At the moment, topics of research in the device independence area include, for example, how to balance independence with the usability of the application. One application may appear as expected in the devices, but the usability experience might not be as satisfying for all of them. What are the steps to create abstract general presentation models? Should generation of the specific presentation models be totally automatic, or just partially so that authors can manipulate it?

Regarding scalability, Roe and Gonik [24] introduces a scalability design process based on a set of useful strategies when designing scalable Internet sites. The strategies are based on the design principles of a scalable architecture: divide and conquer, asynchrony, encapsulation, concurrency and parsimony. A set of guidelines for system partitioning, i.e. dividing the system into components with well-defined interfaces and functionality, is provided. The message is clear: successful wireless Internet services need to be scalable, however, scalability demands a sophisticated architecture, a sophisticated design and, once implemented, requires monitoring and maintenance.

In order to build seamless mobile services, Friday et al. [20] propose techniques that can be used to adapt the system and improve the QoS of the network at different levels i.e. user, application, middleware and transport. For example, the system can allow the user to change from synchronous to asynchronous tasks (user level) or, through proxy services, the application can use local substitute services based on cache information (application level). At the middleware level, the information can be retrieved only when needed (on demand), and finally at the transport level, data can be prioritised, reordered and exchanged according to the current bandwidth situation.

The adaptation techniques were validated through the development of a mobile collaborative system. One of the final conclusions of the study was that mobile systems must have the support of adaptation techniques at all levels in order to be effective, but architectures to propagate QoS information through the system are still required.

A discussion of billing infrastructure and charging models for the actual and future Internet and how they could be modified for being used in wireless Internet services is presented in [25]. A further interesting example is the charging model proposed by Odlyzko [26] which presupposes that the subscriber defines a class as an association between cost and network traffic. First class users have more privileges, e.g., low network delay and low congestion, but must pay more. The user could define the use of the network as first class or second class according to the desired trade-off between network traffic quality and cost.

This model introduces complexity to the network behaviour, overhead to the subscriber and, which is most important for developers, changes to the software application and extensions to the communication protocols. Therefore, developers must ask themselves during the conception of the application's design how much the model of charging and billing impacts the system's architecture.

The usage-centered engineering [28] approach addresses user interface usability as an important factor in design. Designers must produce a role model, a task model and an abstract model; the role model groups the common characteristics of user interaction with the system into roles. These characteristics are related to the purpose, duration, attitude towards the system and information exchange between the user and the system. A task model is a set of task cases and their relationships. A task case lists the steps of the system to provide the desired functionality without assumptions about the user interface. Finally, the abstract model describes the user interface with interaction contexts. The abstract model does not contain details about the look and behaviour of the user interface. Designers use these models to create a comprehensive user interface in which all of them are combined. This comprehensive user interface can be validated by the customer.

More specific guidelines for designing user interfaces can be found for devices or families of devices. The big mobile device producers or programming platform providers offer them, for example, the MIDP style guide offered by Sun Microsystems, Inc [29]. The previous approaches give guidelines for producing usable sites, but how could that be measured? The card sorting technique is proposed by Upchurch et al. [30] for eliciting quality measures of web pages. This technique is based on a personal construct theory whose objective is to elicit and ensure the validity of a measure for a fuzzy attribute like *quality* in a new field such as the Internet. It provides a systematic way to identify quality measures that the stakeholders consider important. In a new domain like the wireless Internet, this can be of great help because it minimises the suppositions about the stakeholder's usability preferences.

2.4 Coding

2.4.1 Guidelines Based on Experience

The purpose of this phase is to produce and integrate the code that implements the design document and, consequently, meets the requirements specification. The basic activities to accomplish this goal are code, code unit test, integrate the code units and release the code (optional).

The activities shown in Figure 2.4 do not differ much from the code activity of any other domain. However, developers found differences originating from the languages to be used for implementing the services.

Pilot 1 was developed based on the assumption that plenty of Internet services for providing financial, weather or sport information is available to clients, i.e. services require little user interaction. These services could in theory, be deployed as wireless devices using the wireless application protocol (WAP). At the moment,

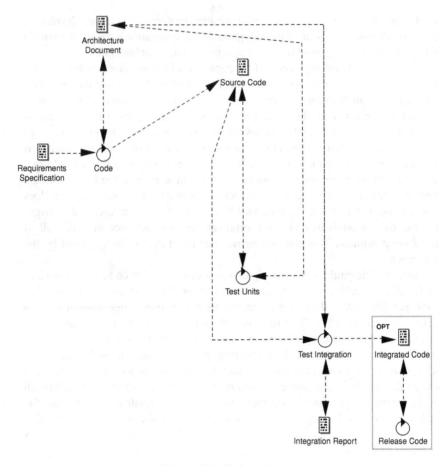

FIGURE 2.4. Coding phase.

the WAP 1.x and 2.0 standards are available [31]. WAP 1.x uses the wireless markup language (WML) for document formatting. WML is a language similar to HTML, specially designed for small clients with small screens and low bandwidth. Complete architecture rework of the service in order to translate HTML into WML was not needed, however, maintenance became a major task because every modification to the HTML version had to be made in the WML version also.

Wireless Internet services that demand interaction with their users, such as games, need a more flexible programming platform. Today some wireless devices can be programmed using some sort of C-like language, but C is not a cross-platform language and therefore, portability among different hardware architectures is lost. A dedicated client should be deployed for every possible platform, delaying time-to-market of the service and increasing costs. JAVA, on the other hand, is commonly used because of its portability. Especially after the release of J2ME, Java can now be deployed on many wireless devices providing a common ground for developers.

Pilot 2 developers used J2ME for implementing a game service. In this case, some devices showed performance problems when the graphics were stored on the client. A proposal for solving this problem was to store the graphics on the server and transfer them to the device on demand. This implied the use of caching algorithms which optimised the performance. Additionally, developers had to optimise the code in order to reduce the amount of storage used by code. Although optimisation, as a side effect, protects the java code from re-engineering [33], optimisers can reduce the size of code by renaming classes, methods and variables in a shorter string. Maintaining such code is hard and fault finding is doubly hard.

The developers who participated in the projects performed their unit tests using emulators for WAP and J2ME. One fact noted after unit testing was that the emulators were not at all realistic regarding the features of the real device. Developers had to produce new code in order to replace functionality provided by the emulator, but non-existent in the real device. Thus, it is suggested that real devices are introduced early on in the development process. The developers performed their unit tests using the "J2ME™ Wireless Toolkit 2.1" which is a client emulator allowing Midlets to run on top of it while emulating the functionality of a mobile device. Specific components such as network modules were tested on cell phones since they were critical for the rest of the application. The graphic library components were tested separately before including them in the application.

2.4.2 Input from Other Work

Pair programming is a technique promoted by eXtreme Programming whereby two developers produce code in one machine [15]. One person concentrates on the strategy to produce the code and the other on whether the approach could work and how it could be simplified. The second one has control of the computer. Pair programming can be seen as difficult to implement in an industrial context but in a new domain such as the wireless Internet it could perhaps have a beneficial effect in order to resolve new and uncertain problems due to its person-to-person communication mechanism.

Zettel et al. [7] propose the LIPE process model to develop e-commerce services on time to market, based on other eXtreme Programming techniques like refactoring.

Although eXtreme Programming techniques seem to be flexible enough, there are some drawbacks. In the case of refactoring, small teams formed of highly experienced developers can be successful [14]. What if the developers are not so experienced? It has been concluded in [10] that eXtreme Programming techniques are not really suited for larger teams. Although success cases for larger teams have been presented [34], this situation must be considered exceptional in the wireless Internet services domain where projects can become large and complex.

To optimise the use of the end device capabilities, tips, guidelines and techniques can be found in the J2ME/WAP developer discussion groups. One example can be found in [32] where security for WAP applications can be assured through the Wireless Transport Layer Security (WTLS). In the case of J2ME applications, power and memory constraints make security a challenge.

WAP 2.0 uses the extensible hypertext markup language (XHTML) for formatting purposes [31]. In theory, WAP2.0 allows developers to create richer applications that handle multimedia and animation amongst other features. Almost all available browsers can display XHTML, but not all HTML features can be converted into XHTML. cHTML is the content development language for i-mode (NTT DoCoMo's Wireless Service). cHTML is similar to HTML but is optimised for wireless networks and devices. More details on the programming languages mentioned above and others are provided in Chapter 3.

2.5 Plan Testing

2.5.1 Guidelines Based on Experience

The purpose of this phase is to produce test cases for each of the requirements specified and set up the hardware and software environment necessary to execute the test cases.

This requires the following activities: planning of the tests to check the structure, functionality, performance, content and usability of the service and setting up the needed hardware and software in order to execute the planned tests (see Figure 2.5).

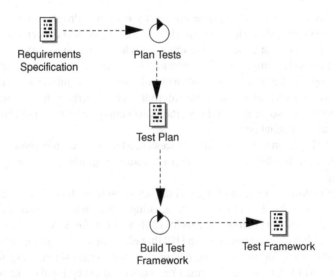

FIGURE 2.5. Plan tests.

The assumption at the beginning of the WISE projects—that setting up a real test environment for the application, i.e., the target device(s), server and network, was a complex task—led to the inclusion of a special activity in the process to accomplish this objective. The effort needed to set up the testing environment of a wireless Internet service is considerable and should not be underestimated.

Finding mechanisms or tools for simulation or emulation can help to solve the problem and reduce costs for setting up a realistic testing environment. Technology providers provide emulators for many mobile devices on the market.

Emulators approximate the functionality of the target device. In practice, using network emulators can be of great help for creating tests, collecting the results and repeating them under different network conditions.

In general, the following issues must be taken into account, especially before setting up the environment for testing a wireless Internet service.

1. Look for a suitable simulator/emulator or design test cases that reflect the behaviour of the network.
2. Make sure that the mobile device is available. If this is not the case, use the device emulators but keep in mind that usually the functionality and API of such emulators may be slightly different from the functionality and API of the target devices.

The developers of the pilot projects performed their unit tests using emulators for WAP and J2ME. They had to produce new code in order to replace functionality provided by the emulator but non-existent in the real device. It is therefore recommended that future projects should try to introduce the use of real devices as early as possible in the development process. This activity was considered to be of great relevance by the developers of the pilots especially because there are hidden risks (e.g., high costs, lack of suitable technology) that could make a project fail. A list of basic steps to 'build a test framework' has been to set-up a test environment has been included in Chapter 5 with the name "built test framework".

2.5.2 Input from Other Work

Markov models [44] are mathematical models that can be used for the validation of the mobile application's usability. This mathematical construct is based on finite state machines and can be helpful in analysing the usability applications implemented in push button devices such as mobile phones or PDAs. Finite state machines represent the whole system as a set of states and transitions and are particularly effective at modelling, as they are simple, quick to produce and scalable to any size. As well-defined mathematical objects, it is possible to perform complex reasoning on the model to produce reproducible, quantitative results.

A sophisticated technique to plan the tests of wireless Internet services is the model-based testing technique [41]. Similarly as Markov models, this technique also uses finite state machines and directed graphs or state transition diagrams as a basis for creating models to test the functionality of the application. Benefits of model-based testing include the written structure of states and transitions and the possibility of automating tests, giving a general understanding to all team members on how the application should work. It is still a topic of research to find out if model-based testing is a cost-appropriate technique for finding defects, due to the fact that the effort invested by developers on building the model is not negligible.

Central-control wireless emulators abstract the entire mobile wireless network to a model with a set of parameters thus emulating end-to-end applications and protocols. The emulator applies network conditions and traffic dynamics to each packet passing by to reproduce the network effects, thereby testing the performance of the applications and protocols. This type of emulation is conducted by connecting mobile hosts such as handheld devices and computers to the central-control emulator. Examples of such emulators are ONE [35] and Dummynet [36].

VINT/NS [37] is one of the commonly used simulation combined wireless emulators. The emulation facility in VINT/NS is able to capture and direct traffic into the simulator. Within the simulator, protocol modules, algorithms and visualisation tools can be incorporated in an automatic fashion. In addition, arbitrary mobility can be generated with the help of the simulator. Its advantage is that it offers a large amount of simulation resources in the central simulator, compared with the central-control approach that only has a limited number of network parameters available. However, this approach lacks support for the evaluation of real topology related protocols.

The trace-based mobile network emulator [38] also emulates characteristics such as performance and bandwidth in a real environment. The flying emulator [39] emulates the physical mobility of wireless devices it can test software designed to run on a wireless device in the same way as if the software were disconnected from the network, moved with the device and reconnected to and then operated on another network.

One distributed network emulator system, EMPOWER [40], provides a mechanism to emulate the mobility of a wireless network in a wireline network. EMPOWER allows the user to define packet latency and bandwidth as parameters and test a given topology wireless network.

2.6 Testing

2.6.1 Guidelines Based on Experience

The purpose of this phase is to execute the planned test cases and validate that the specified requirements are met by the service implementation. As observed in Figure 2.6, the mandatory activity is the system test, while the rest is optional.

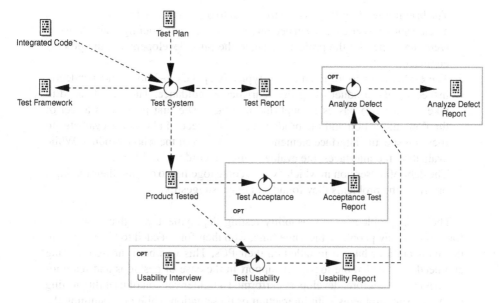

FIGURE 2.6. Testing phase.

The reasons for identifying these other activities as optional were based on the following:

1. Even though the activity 'test usability' is very important, it was declared optional since it demands effort and resources (as observed in the WISE project) that some organisations cannot afford.
2. The 'acceptance test' was declared optional as it demands close collaboration and good communication channels between the customer and the developer which cannot always be realised.
3. Finally, the activity 'analyse defect' was declared optional because, in the context of the WISE project, the most mature partners did follow it, while the less mature ones did not.

The complete functionality of the system (client and server) was tested using the real environment when both real devices and emulators were used. Tests on the real device alone were more time-consuming. One example was to test what happened when the application was interacting with other phones and a call came in, or when the battery went dead.

The activity 'test usability' is based on the paper by Nielsen [50] in which experts, guided by a set of usability heuristics, evaluate whether user-interface elements such as dialogue boxes, menus, navigation structure, online help, etc. conform to user needs. The activity consists of the following sessions:

1. The briefing session: Experts are told what to do. A prepared script is useful as a guide and to ensure that each person receives the same briefing. The heuristics were developed by the project manager, the pilot developers and the process engineer.
2. The evaluation period: Each expert typically spends 1–2 hours independently inspecting the product using the heuristics as guidance. The experts need to take at least two passes through the interface. The first pass gives a feel of the flow interaction and the product scope, the second allows the evaluator to focus on specific interface elements in the context of the whole product. While evaluating the interfaces, the evaluator must record the problems.
3. The debriefing session in which experts come together to discuss their findings, prioritise the problems they found and make suggestions.

The main problem of the usability testing deployment was that it was performed by many people at the same time, who therefore needed to have access to the application or have it installed on their PCs. This was both time-consuming and needed considerable logistical support in the case of desktops and real mobile devices. Therefore, developers performed a lighter version of usability testing once they saw problems with interaction or presentation while programming the graphical user interface. A list of usability items was recorded and used to improve the user interface. Examples of how this information was recorded are given below.

USABILITY PROBLEM 1

Issue. The 'Logged in the game community' screen does not show enough information. It is not clear which user is logged in and if a character has been loaded or not.
Solution. Add such information below the bottom icons, in a space that is already used as status bar.

USABILITY PROBLEM 2

Issue. When starting a new game, a presentation of the situation could help. Otherwise, the player feels lost and without aim.
Solution. Add a dialogue and content for it. A great part of the presentation dialogue can be reused for this implementation.

USABILITY PROBLEM 3

Issue. When a user is hit, he/she does not have the impression of being hit. The display of server notifications is really poor.
Solution. Add a damage image and sound and also improve the event notifications. The Dungeon Master will notify the players of the game event or actions (i.e., 'You have been damaged').

2.6.1.1 Input from Other Work

The usability of mobile devices as a medium to deploy WAP applications has been criticised because of their physical limitations by Nielsen [46]. Their usability test and studies reveal that bigger and more capable user displays improve user interfaces and therefore acceptance by users. An interesting study done by Buchanan et al. [47] was focused on detecting usability problems through testing and afterwards improving the application. In this study, the users tested alternatives of a user interface with the same functionality. A group of users were assembled and then performed the same activities within a wireless Internet service. Meanwhile the time and number of interactions were measured. Finally, users were interviewed about their experiences and suggestions. The measures and information were taken as a basis for deciding the most suitable interface and for creating guidelines to be used in future projects. Looking at the previous references can help software managers and developers to better understand the user's problems when interacting with mobile devices.

The web usability assessment model [43] includes 11 usability attributes which had been identified as significant in assessing a customer's perceived usability. The usability attributes include design layout, navigation, personalisation, design consistency, design standards, reliability, security, performance, information content, accessibility and customer service. An automated usability testing tool named usability enforcer tool based on the web usability assessment model implements a set of usability rules for a targeted customer profile, the specified computing environment and the strategic goals of the wireless application.

One visualisation-based approach to improve the usability of a web site and a predictive model to locate problem areas is introduced by Chi [42]. The approach underlines the importance of using visualisation techniques to understand the behaviour of users on a web site and to identify unreachable places. Visualisation techniques can also be used to analyse the past behaviour of a site and to understand the impact of new changes.

The software that runs on mobile devices can also be validated against the amount of power consumed by the components of the device when the application is in use [45]. Applications interact not only with the display, but also with various other hardware devices: processor, memory, network interface and possibly hard drive. All these devices consume energy during operation. This gives an opportunity to monitor and record power levels during the test suite execution.

2.7 Life Cycle Process Models

This section provides a brief discussion of life cycle process models that are commonly referenced in the software engineering literature and that may be suitable for developing wireless Internet services.

The throwaway prototype model and the incremental development model [3], which were found suitable for domains of similar characteristics like the Internet and mobile phones [4]–[9] prescribe to provide initially essential operational functions and then add more advanced and sophisticated versions of the system. Increments are usually defined as an agreement between the customer and the development organisation. This allows development organisations to get feedback from the final customer during the development of the increments until the final version of the solution is delivered. Additionally, monitoring and controlling the project plan can be done more precisely and the quality of increments can be assured with the established verification and validation activities.

Agile development practices and techniques aim at finding a balance between flexibility and structure in the actual business environment, where volatility and uncertainty increase [10], [11]. One of them, adaptive software development (ASD), proposes tackling uncertainty by means of short delivery iterations; new requirements and technical information with intensive collaboration among managers, customers and developers and process improvement with reviews and project retrospectives after each iteration.

The dynamic systems development method (DSDM) [10] contains three major phases of iteration: functional model iteration, design and build iteration, and implementation iteration. DSDM is similar to ASD because it allows the introduction of new functionality (new requirements) late in the project. Additionally, prototypes built for each feature are preferred over long documents as documentation.

One risk of agile approaches is that they rely on the tacit knowledge and experience of developers [12]. Moreover, issues like scalability and performance have to be carefully designed.

The spiral model [13] assumes risks as the driving force of software projects. This model proposes ongoing refinement of the system specification into source code components. Refinements are made through cycles and each cycle is risk assessed. A risk assessment determines if a project continues or is to be cancelled or redefined. The nature of the spiral model seems reasonable to apply in an unstable domain like wireless but the real cost of identifying, analysing and maintaining risks can be high, which is not feasible for small- and medium-sized companies.

Boehm [14] proposes a combination of agile and plan-driven methods through the risk-driven spiral method, which is intended to balance flexibility and discipline. The rationale behind this is that although the market changes constantly and puts pressure on development organisations to deliver their products rapidly, increasing dependability of systems and applications demands high quality products.

2.8 Conclusions

The reference process model presented in this chapter, although it does not differ significantly from traditional iterative process models at the life cycle level, provides a deeper insight into the wireless characteristics that must be evaluated by project managers and developers before and during the implementation of wireless Internet services. The representation of alternative and optional parts provides the basis for a better understanding of the possible options for developing wireless Internet services, taking into account the context of the project. For instance, it is now known that planning the tests of wireless Internet services can be a complicated task, influenced by the heterogeneity of devices and networks. Therefore, it is seen as an optional task for small software development organisations, which may not have enough budget to invest in this. On the other hand, by leaving aside this activity, software managers and developers know the risk and must look for contingency plans to mitigate it, e.g., the negotiation of testing facilities before signing the contract. There is also the view that without this activity, the product will be less than professional.

Many hints were provided not only from various literature sources but also from the experiences of pilot projects that summarised the most important points to take into account for new projects.

One outstanding observation was the need to perform design feasibility studies in order to better understand the technology and the possibilities for implementing a service. Experiences from the pilots showed that the requirements phase was difficult to control due to the novelty of the domain and the fact that low level requirements and, particularly, usability related requirements, e.g., how to represent large tables on small displays, were often not well understood. Feasibility studies proved to be a good means to handle the related uncertainty.

Testing proved very challenging due to the great diversity of devices available on the market, the unreliability of device specifications, the low degree of automation of the testing procedures on real devices and the unreliability of the available emulators.

References

1. Kovari, P., Acker, V.B., Marino, A., Ryan, J., Tang, L.K., Weiss, C.: Mobile Applications with Websphere Everyplace Access Design and Development. IBM SG24-6259-00 (2001).
2. Buttler, M.H.: Current Technologies for Device Independence. HP Laboratories, HP-2001-83, Bristol, UK (2001).
3. McDermid, J.A., Rook, P.: *Software Development Process Models, Software Engineer's Reference Book*. Boca Raton, FL: CRC Press, pp. 15.26–15.28 (1994).
4. Adamopoulos, D.X., Pavlou, G., Papandreou, C.A.: An integrated and systematic approach for the development of telematic services in heterogeneous distributed platforms. *Computer Communications*, Vol. 24, pp. 294–315 (2001).
5. Karlsson, E., Taxen, L.: Incremental development for AXE 10. ACM SIGSOFT Software Engineering Notes, Vol. 22, no. 6 (1997).
6. Taylor, M.J., McWilliam, J., Forsyth, H., Wade, S.: Methodologies and website development: A survey of practice. *Information and Software Technology*, Vol. 44, no. 6, pp. 381–391 (2002).

7. Zettel, J., Maurer, M., Münch, J., Wong, L.: LIPE: A Lightweight process for e-business startup companies based on extreme programming. *Proceedings of the Third International Conference on Product-Focused Software Processes Improvement* (PRO-FES), pp. 255–270 (2001).
8. Nilsson, A., Anselmsson, M., Olsson, K., Johansson, Erik.: Impacts of measurement on an SPI program. Q-Labs (http://www.q-labs.com/files/Papers/ SPI99_Imp_of_Meas_on_SPI.pdf).
9. Yau, V.: Project management strategies and practices for wireless CDMA software development. *Proceedings of the IEEE International Conference on Industrial Technology* (1996).
10. Highsmith, J.: What is agile software development? *The Journal of Defense Software Engineering*, Vol. 15, no. 10, October (2002).
11. Maurer, F., Martel, S.: Rapid development for web-based applications. *IEEE Internet Computing*, Vol. 6, no. 1, pp. 86–90 (2002).
12. Boehm, B.W.: Get ready for agile methods, with care. *IEEE Computer*, Vol. 35, no. 1, pp. 64–69 (2002).
13. Boehm, B.W.: A spiral model for software development and enhancement. *IEEE Computer*, Vol. 21, no. 5, pp. 61–72 (1988).
14. Boehm, B.W.: Get ready for agile methods, with care. *IEEE Computer*, Vol. 35, no. 1, pp. 64–69 (2002).
15. Beck, K.: *Extreme Programming Explained: Embrace Change*. MA Boston, USA: Addison Wesley, (2000).
16. Constantine, L.L., Lockwood, A.D.L.: Usage-centered engineering for web applications. *IEEE Software*, Vol. 19, no. 2, pp. 42–50 (2002).
17. Hammar, C.M.: Designing user-centred web applications in web time. *IEEE Software*, Vol. 18, no. 1, pp. 62–69 (2001).
18. http://www.w3.org/TR/2001/WD-di-princ-20010918/
19. Schwabe, D., Mattos, G.R., Rossi, G.: Cohesive design of personalized web applications. *IEEE Internet Computing*, Vol. 6, no. 2, pp. 34–43 (2002).
20. Friday, A., Davies, N., Blair, G.S., Cheverest, K.W.J.: Developing adaptive applications: The MOST experience. *Integrated Computer Aided Engineering: ICAE*, Vol. 6, no. 2, pp. 143–158 (1999).
21. Giannetti, F.: Device independency web application framework. *W3C Device Independent Authoring Techniques Workshop*, pp. 25–26 (2002).
22. Wong, C., Chu, H., Katagiri M.: A single authoring technique for building device independent presentations. *W3C Device Independent Authoring Techniques Workshop* (2002).
23. Mori, G., Paterno, F., Santono, C.: An XML based approach for designing nomadic applications. *W3C Device Independent Authoring Techniques Workshop* (2002).
24. Roe, C., Gonik, S.: Server-side design principles for scalable Internet systems. *IEEE Software*, Vol. 19, no. 2, pp. 34–41 (2002).
25. Cushnie, J., Hutchison, D., Oliver, H.: Evolution of charging and billing models for GSM and future mobile Internet services. Lecture Notes in Computer Science, Vol. 1922, pp. 312–323 (2000).
26. Odlyzko, A.: Paris Metro Pricing: The Minimalist Differentiated Services Solution. *Proceedings of the Seventh IEEE/IFIP International Workshop on Quality of Service (IWQoS)*, pp. 159–161 (1999).

27. Wong, C., Chu, H., Katagiri, M.: GUI migration across heterogeneous Java profiles. *Proceedings of ACM SIGCHI-NZ'02* (2002).
28. Constantine, L.L., Lockwood, A.D.L.: Usage-centred engineering for web applications. *IEEE Software*, Vol. 19, no. 2, pp. 42–50 (2002).
29. http://java.sun.com/j2me/docs/alt-html/midp-style-guide7/preface.html
30. Upchurch, L., Rugg, G., Kitchenham, B.: Using card sorts to elicit web page quality attributes. *IEEE Software*, Vol. 18, no. 4, pp. 84–89 (2002).
31. Read, K., Maurer, F.: Developing mobile wireless applications. *IEEE Internet Computing*, Vol. 7, no. 1, pp. 81–86 (2003).
32. http://wireless.java.sun.com/midp/tips/appsize/
33. Colberg, C.S., Thomborson, C.: Watermarking, tamperproofing and obfuscation- tools for software protection. *IEEE Transactions on Software Engineering*, Vol. 28, no. 8, pp. 735–746 (2002).
34. Cockburn, A., Highsmith, J.: Agile software development: The people factor. *Computer*, Vol. 34, no. 11, pp. 131–133 (2001).
35. Kohler, E., Morris, R., Chen, B., Jannotti, J., Kaashoek M.F.: The click modular router. *Proceedings of ACM Transactions on Computer Systems*, Vol. 18, pp. 263–297, (2000).
36. Rizzo, L.: Dummynet: a simple approach to the evaluation of network protocols. *Proceedings of ACM Computer Communication Review*, Vol. 27 (1997).
37. Fall, K.: Network emulation in the VINT/NS simulator, *Proceedings of 4th IEEE Symposium on Computers and Communications*, (1999).
38. Noble, B.D., Satyanarayanan, M., Giao, T.N, Katz, H.R.: Trace-based mobile network emulation. *Proceedings of the ACM SIGCOMM '97 conference on Applications, Technologies, Architectures and Protocols for Computer Communication.*
39. Satoh, I.: Flying emulator: rapid building and testing of networked applications for mobile computers, *Proceedings of 5th International Conference on Mobile Agents* (MA'2001), Lecture Notes in Computer Science (LNCS), London, UK, Vol. 2240, pp. 103–118, Springer (2001).
40. Zheng, P., Ni, M.N.: EMPOWER: A network emulator for wireless and wireline networks. *Proceedings of IEEE INFOCOM* (2003).
41. El-Far, I.K., Thompson, H,H., Mottay, F.E.: Experiences in testing pocket PC applications. *Proceedings of the Fifth International Software and Internet Quality Week Europe* (2002).
42. Chi, E.: Improving web usability through visualization. *IEEE Internet Computing*, Vol. 6, no. 2, pp. 64–71 (2002).
43. Becker, S., Mottay, F.: A Global Perspective on Web Site Usability, IEEE Software, Vol. 18, no. 1, pp. 54–61 (2001).
44. Thimbleby H., Cairns, P., Jones M.: Usability analysis with markov models. *ACM Transactions on Computer-Human Interaction*, Vol. 8 (2001).
45. Sinha, A., Chandrakasan, A.: JouleTrack—A web based tool for software energy profiling. *Proceedings of the 38th Design Automation Conference* (2001).
46. Nielsen, J.: Graceful degradation of scalable internet services, WAP: Wrong approach to portability, alertbox 31/10/1999 at http://www.useit.com/alertbox/991031.html
47. Buchanan, G., Farrant, S., Jones, M., Thimbleby, H., Marsden, G., Pazzani, M.J.: Improving mobile internet usability. *Proceedings World Wide Web* 10, pp. 673–680, (2001).
48. Becker-Kornstaedt, U., Hamann, D., Kempkens, R., Rösch, P., Verlage, M., Webby, R., Zettel, J.: Support for the process engineer: The spearmint approach to software

process definition and process guidance. *Proceedings of the Eleventh Conference on Advanced Information Systems Engineering (CAISE '99)*, pp. 119–133. Lecture Notes in Computer Science, Springer-Verlag: Berlin Heidelberg, New York (1999).

49. Becker-Kornstaedt, U., Boggio, D., Muench, J., Ocampo, A., Palladino, Gino.: Empirically driven design of software development processes for wireless Internet services. *Proceedings of the Fourth International Conference on Product-Focused Software Processes Improvement (PROFES)* (2002).

50. Nielsen, J., Mack, R.L.: *Usability Inspection Methods* New York: John Wiley & Sons, Inc (1994).

3
Technology

MARIO NEGRO PONZI, HEIMO LAAMANEN

The main goal of this chapter, which is an overview of available programming technologies for wireless devices, is to show developers the advantages and disadvantages of each technology.

This chapter does not provide a complete technological description but provides an overview and some hopefully useful suggestions.

New technologies will soon make today's leading edge concepts obsolete. The approach taken in this chapter, however, will still be useful because it first focuses on network technologies and then goes on to multiple client solutions. Existing families will grow up and perhaps new families will arise but it will be a matter of evolution instead of revolution. Basic classification (thin vs. fat clients) and cross-platform approaches are seen as being stable concepts.

The chapter starts by describing the wireless environment; it then provides a technical overview of both networks and devices and finally, it delves into available development environments.

Again, this is by no means an in-depth technological description: readers interested in tutorials or references concerning a particular solution or device should refer to specific technical documents (see links at the end of this chapter).

The technologies described are available worldwide but it must be stressed that some differences can be found in the main market areas which are taken to be Europe, America and Japan. Some technologies, such as iMode [9], are not widely available outside their reference market.

3.1 The Environment

Today's distributed systems often based on the client–server paradigm are typically designed and implemented to work in the environment of fixed data networks. In particular, the QoS requirements of distributed systems, especially those related to reliability, require a reliable and predictable transport and data communications service. In the Internet and intranets, the trustworthiness of the transport services is achieved by using the TCP/IP protocols. However, TCP/IP, as used in the wired world, may not be adequate for applications in the environment of wireless data communications.

Wireless data communications are by their nature different from wireline data communications and mobile hosts differ from stationary hosts in a number of respects. The behaviour of data transmission services offered by wireline and wireless data networks differ greatly and in several different respects:

Firstly, in wireless data communications, QoS parameter values such as line rate, delay, throughput, round-trip time and error rate may change rapidly and dramatically as a mobile end-user moves from one location to another. For example, when the nomadic end-user roams from a UMTS (Universal Mobile Telecommunications System) cell to a GPRS cell, the throughput may drop from 384 kbps down to 24 Kbps, or in the reverse case, the throughput may increase from 24 Kbps up to 384 kbps. The reason for this is the movement of mobiles across regions where radio signals take different path from the transmitter getting in and out of regions of cancellation and reinforcement of the signal, are the main reasons for the features above.

Secondly, the variety of mobile devices (such as portable PCs, hand-held devices and smart phones) that mobile end-users will use to access Internet services is increasing rapidly. For example, smart phones just cannot display high-quality images which are designed to be displayed on the screens of high-end laptop PCs. Therefore it is unwise to transfer such images over low throughput wireless links especially when nomadic end-users must pay to receive data which they cannot take advantage of.

Thus, the environment of distributed systems made up of mobile hosts and wireless data communications introduces new features and aspects to the designers and programmers of such systems. Dependability is one of the factors that requires special attention. The new features and aspects affect both availability (readiness for usage) and reliability (continuity of service) of the services of distributed systems. In the case of availability, on one hand, wireless data communications extend the availability of services to geographical areas where the services cannot be offered using wireline data communications; on the other hand, wireless data communications are more untrustworthy than wireline data communications. The typical fault types in wireless and wireline data communications are different. For example, failures may be caused by a temporary interference to a radio signal or by a mobile end-user trying to access a service outside of the coverage area of a wireless data communication network. Recovery actions therefore are different. In the first case, just waiting for a short period recovers the situation and in the second case the end-user can carry out the recovery action by changing his or her location. The reliability of a service is more variable and dependent on nomadic end-users' own actions, e.g., motion, than it is in the environment consisting of stationary hosts and fixed data networks. Time and place affect the environment of systems of wireless data communications and mobile hosts more than systems of stationary hosts and fixed data networks. These issues should be taken into account in the development of applications. Recovery actions are, in many cases, application-specific.

The inherent flexibility and adaptability of today's distributed systems are normally unable to reliably deliver services in an environment of changing QoS, availability and reliability. It can be argued that for wireless data communications it is impossible to obtain a guaranteed end-to-end communication path. There is often a clear on–off situation: the services of mobile distributed systems are either available or unavailable. This will not be satisfactory for mobile end-users who will usually expect to receive the best obtainable service on every occasion. Future mobile distributed systems need to provide these users with several levels of service depending on the current wireless environment. The levels of the services need to establish a contiguous spectrum of QoS for the services of mobile distributed systems.

3.2 Wireless Networks Overview

It is important to get a picture of wireless networks capabilities (bandwidth, latency, etc.) since they strongly influence what an application can and cannot achieve. For example, a multiplayer real-time networked game has such strict requirements on network delay that some networks simply cannot deliver an adequate QoS. In this case developers will probably have to refocus on a turn-based game that has lower QoS needs.

3.2.1 The IR Preamble

Infrared communications is the first example of widely available wireless data communications for hand-held mobile devices and notebooks.[1] Today, the vast majority of mobile phones have an IR communication port and, while not considered as a proper wireless standard,[2] it is worth mentioning that some very important application protocols (such as OBEX) have been standardised to be used with IR [26], and only later they have been moved to other technologies such as Bluetooth.

3.2.2 Bluetooth

Bluetooth is a PAN (personal area network) standard which has reached the mass market through wireless earphones for mobile phones and, to a lesser extent, for data synchronisation (PDAs and similar). It is now available as an industrial RS232 replacement and even in remote home-theatre speakers, in car hands-free devices,

---

[1] Here radio modems are ignored since they were never widely adopted outside specific companies and specialists.

[2] IR is not considered a concrete usable wireless protocol because it needs proper device visual alignment and, more important, it just connects two devices not allowing any kind of structured 'network' link. However it is still an easy choice for data synchronisation among devices.

etc. Today, Bluetooth, which started life in an industrial forum called the Bluetooth Special Interest Group, has been standardised by the IEEE as 802.15.1 and there are high- and low-speed variants called WiMedia and ZigBee respectively. When Bluetooth was standardised, the main requirements were low range, low cost and low energy consumption suitable for battery-powered devices.

Bluetooth features:

- a 10-m range (with longer range versions on the market);
- a maximum bandwidth of 768 kbps;
- a limited amount of contemporary connected devices: Bluetooth networks (called *piconets*) cannot support more than eight devices.[3] Multiple piconets in an area are called scatternets and
- extreme resistance to interference.

The above attributes clearly identify the kind of wireless support Bluetooth was designed to provide.

From a programmer's perspective, the protocol is not a 'simple' protocol. The Bluetooth protocol is built in layers. Users do not have to worry about the low-level details as devices ship with a set of supported *profiles*, which identify the typical use(s) of the device. Every device has to support the GAP (Generic Access Profile), which ensures basic interoperability.

Profiles support synchronous communications (very low latency communications without too much concern for packet loss), useful for real-time audio transmission, or asynchronous data transfers, useful for data synchronisation.

Common profiles include headset, hands-free, audio gateway as well as Serial Communication Profile, network and others.

The 'profile' approach was intended to simplify programmers' lives, but lack of standardisation in APIs and hardware from manufacturers slows down development.

To address security issues [2], it is mandatory that Bluetooth devices, prior to starting communications, *pair*. This means that each device should be explicitly allowed to use another's services through the exchange of a password. Bluetooth devices should be set in the *discoverable* mode before pairing can take place.

Data transmission has to be encrypted as in every wireless link. Detailed information about Bluetooth security can be found in [1].

The protocol is evolving so that new devices have a range of 100 m and have a user data rate of about 10 times the current one. All these advantages come at the expense of power consumption.

---

[3] Bluetooth spec allows for a total of eight devices (one master plus seven slaves) per piconet, and that this is a direct limitation of the 3-bit address field. However the limitation is seven active slaves per piconet. There can be any number of parked slaves in a piconet (up to 255 that are directly addressable by a parked slave address). The master can 'swap out' active slaves.

3.2.3 Wi-Fi

While Bluetooth has been designed to replace 'short' wires, i.e., those for head-phones, speakers and the like, wireless LANs (local area networks) such as IEEE 802.11b have been designed to replace LAN office cabling. It was designed for high bandwidth and compatibility with existing wired LAN standards (Ethernet). This WLAN is often referred to by the name of the industry group promoting interoperability, Wi-Fi, which stands for wireless fidelity.

Typical numbers of a Wi-Fi link are:

- About 100-m range: as for Bluetooth, the effective range inside urban areas and indoors is much shorter;
- Maximum bandwidth of about 11 Mbps (up to 108 Mbps with newer protocol variants such as dual 802.11g) and
- Support for medium-size networks: typical Wi-Fi access points support up to 256 devices.

As mentioned above, the Wi-Fi standard was designed to integrate and/or replace wired LANs. Wi-Fi devices are then connected with Ethernet networks using access points. This operation mode is called *infrastructure* and it is the most typical use of Wi-Fi. There is also a point-to-point mode for enabling a direct link between two devices without access point support (called *ad-hoc*).

In Wi-Fi, authentication is implemented recognising MAC addresses while security is implemented using a dedicated WEP (Wireless Encryption Privacy) protocol. Both systems have been criticised for being insecure (MAC addresses can be spoofed and the WEP protocol can be easily broken, see [4–7]) so that this protocol cannot be taken seriously for security. A new security system for WLANs is much stronger. Security may also be addressed at an application level or using systems like IPSec.

Wi-Fi and Bluetooth technologies were designed to solve different needs but they have evolved so much that they now partially overlap. Today, the main differences are power consumption, which is far lower in Bluetooth and network capabilities, which are usually better using Wi-Fi because of the more computer-oriented approach; the main Wi-Fi advantage is that network-based applications do not have to be rewritten to support the protocol (efforts are undergoing to add a TCP/IP layer for Bluetooth). Both need external support to achieve strong security.

3.2.4 Mobile Phone Networks: from GSM to UMTS

While Bluetooth and Wi-Fi are found in personal and local networks, the biggest market is WAN wireless networks.

In this area, voice wireless network operators are pushing technology from voice to data transmission in a way similar to that adopted some years ago by wired network operators that began to transmit data using analogue modems and then via ISDN and now xDSL (broadband).

Initially, GSM services had very limited data transmission offering only a bandwidth of 9.6 kbps, but new standards like GPRS have emerged and others like EDGE (enhanced data for GSM evolution) and UMTS are in the deployment phase.

Briefly, mobile phones are classified in 'generations', the first generation was represented by mobile analogue systems such as TACS/ETACS and AMPS, the second is represented by digital systems, mainly GSM with other systems like DAMPS and CDMAOne, whereas the third is that of digital systems supporting the exchange of multimedia streams. The main third generation technology is UMTS. Between the second and third generations lies a middle generation that targets data transmission on second generation mobile networks without a full technological change. Below is a brief description of today's technologies suitable for data transmission.

3.2.4.1 2.5G: GPRS

GPRS is a kind of sum of many GSM channels (depending on device and network availability) called *slots*: it reaches an asymmetrical wired-modem like downlink bandwidth, with a lower uplink bandwidth (typically that of a single GSM connection). It is widely supported because it does not require the operators to change base stations (just to upgrade software). The cost for installing SGSNs and GGSNs, while high, is justified because the same devices will become the core for 3G networks.

GPRS latency is much higher compared to that of a wired connection because data has to cross wireless to wired network borders.

3.2.4.2 2.5G EDGE

EDGE is compatible with existing GSM networks and gives up to three times GPRS' speeds. Below is a performance comparison with GPRS.

	Peak network speed	Peak device speed	Average PC browser speed (loaded network)	Average streaming media speed (loaded network)
GPRS	60 kbps	53 kbps	20–30 kbps	10–20 kbps
EDGE	180 kbps	180 kbps	80–130 kbps	20–40 kbps

From the table, one could guess why EDGE is not as widely available as GPRS. There are two answers:

1. Although EDGE requires no hardware changes to be made in GSM core networks, base stations must be modified. An EDGE compatible transceiver unit must be installed and the base station system needs to be upgraded to support

EDGE. New mobile terminal hardware and software is also required to de-code/encode using a new radio modulation scheme.[4]

2. European operators are willing to completely skip EDGE in favour of UMTS.

For both reason, it is not easy to find EDGE implementations. However, some US and European operators started deploying it in 2003.

3.2.4.3 3G: UMTS and W-CDMA Variants

Video and data streams need more bandwidth than GSM/GPRS can provide. To resolve this, a new mobile system, UMTS, is being deployed. UMTS requires a complete change in the base station infrastructure whilst basing the core network on GPRS.

UMTS was part of an effort to standardise the world mobile market on a single wireless protocol. That effort (IMT 2000) failed so now UMTS is one of a set of different (and often incompatible) standards. However, at the application level, differences are mostly hidden to the developer.

The biggest problem for application developers, however, is that the maximum bandwidth can be reached only by reducing network cell size. In practice, a UMTS cell should have a range of a few hundred metres. It is economically unfeasible for operators to provide so many base stations to allow high-bandwidth data transmissions. Today, we have UMTS networks delivering 384 kbps to users, unfortunately to only a few users in a cell. Higher speed additions to UMTS such as HSDPA (high-speed downlink packet access) will provide several megabits/second to users.

3.3 Hardware

It is very difficult to classify hardware devices in a rapidly evolving world like the wireless one. Every classification makes sense only until new devices reach the market. New CPUs, batteries with bigger capacities, touch screens, all these change what wireless devices can do. As an example, today, high-end mobile phones ship with text editors and spreadsheets so that they can be used as small PCs. Boundaries between desktop computers, notebooks and PDA are becoming blurred.

While impossible to strictly classify each device, some *reference families* can nonetheless be identified. Usually software targets a specific group of people that

---

[4] Instead of employing GMSK (Gaussian minimum-shift keying), EDGE additionally uses 8PSK (8 Phase Shift Keying), producing a 3-bit word for every change in carrier phase. This effectively triples the gross data rate offered by GSM. EDGE, like GPRS, uses a rate adaptation algorithm that adapts the modulation and coding scheme (MCS) used to improve the quality of the radio channel, and thus the bit rate and robustness of data transmission. It introduces a new technology not found in GPRS, Incremental Redundancy, which, instead of retransmitting disturbed packets, sends more redundancy information to be combined in the receiver. This increases the probability of correct decoding (source: http://en.wikipedia.org).

uses a certain range of devices which identify the family to be selected; technical commonalities have to be identified so that, for example, if a programming language is available on every device of the family, the developer will be able to write a single application using that language or, at least, to develop some shared libraries or components resulting in a shortened time to market.

3.3.1 Families

As mobile devices evolve, there is a convergence between two originally separate technology areas. Firstly, the computer world through PDAs and notebooks and secondly the mobile phones world. Computer manufacturers are trying to reduce the size of their desktops while migrating to wireless connections that will do the job of today's wired LAN while at the same time phone manufacturers are trying to enhance the capabilities of their devices, integrating them with already existing telephone wireless connections.

In the middle are notebooks, sub-notebooks, tablet PCs, PDAs, PDA phones, smart phones, mobile phones, hand-held PCs and others. It is difficult to clearly assign a device to a class: every new device shares features from many categories. However, three families can be identified. Devices belonging to each family share a common technical behaviour.

3.3.1.1 Mobile Phones

It is often difficult to distinguish between 'simple' cellphones and PDA phones (described later) as they both are sold in the same shops and called 'phones' generically. However, a PDA phone is a programmable device that allows the programmer to interact with the operating system (OS), while in mobile phones, programmers are strictly limited in what they can do and cannot interfere with (or even access) the rest of the device (system software libraries, hardware or applications).

Usually mobile phones are much less expensive than PDA phones and therefore they have a huge market-place, and developers targeting a mass market should try to develop for this kind of device. Programming for PDA phones should be left out for business applications or other selected markets for the inverse reason.

A major concern for manufacturers producing mass market devices is to limit the ability for bad or malicious code to damage other applications' data. Because of this, developers' code may face the restriction of running in a *sandbox*. This is clearly not true for developers having special agreements with phone manufacturers as they can access native OS libraries and memory areas.

Since traditionally, almost every cellphone OS has been proprietary and kept secret, manufacturers have looked for an agreement on a common programming platform that could be opened to third-party developers. The most successful results are Internet technologies such as WML (wireless markup language) and J2ME (both described in the software part of this chapter) but deep differences in hardware and OSs still lead to some peculiarities. Proprietary extensions, for example, cause confusion and problems. Physical differences among devices enforce a minimum common denominator approach that is seldom fully satisfying.

Considering hardware, mobile phones can be identified by having

- a numeric keypad;
- some additional buttons to quickly select frequently used functions and
- a 4-way button (or a small joystick) to move across system menus.

They may provide some additional capabilities:

- phone camera: both still and short video clip;
- music support of FM radio or internal card reader for music and
- Bluetooth and infrared capabilities for headphones and PC synchronisation.

As the programming capability of third-party developers matures, allowing the sandbox to be removed, we effectively move into a world of PDA phones.

3.3.1.2 PDAs

PDAs are an extreme form of PC. They are a mix between an electronic diary and a notebook. Typical applications are small databases, on-site computing support for engineers and location-based services such as navigation, provided GPS facilities are available.

The archetypical and best-known PDA family is from Palm. Palm was one of the first successful hand-held device companies together with Psion. It is a fully programmable electronic diary with no keyboard, using instead an area, called the *graffiti* area, where the user is able to draw characters for input using specific symbols. This was because the device was unable to recognise letters requiring more than one stroke (such as an 'i' that requires the user to draw a line and a point). Psion, on the other hand, chose a more traditional approach incorporating a thin keyboard. Today, Psion has switched to industrial wireless devices incorporating Windows CE and sold its share in the Symbian consortium which supported and owned the EPOC OS that was the base for the Symbian OS used on smart phones (see below at PDA phones).[5]

Another actor in the PDA market is Microsoft that developed its Windows CE solution, pushing hardware manufacturers like HP and Compaq to adopt it. Windows CE is a stripped down and customised version of the Windows NT OS. It supports both keyboard-based (initially called hand-held PC) devices and touch-screen devices (initially called PalmPC and then PocketPC to distinguish them from Palm devices). Now they are usually called PocketPC.

Instead of using a dedicated area for input, Windows CE draws a virtual keyboard on the screen. Today, however, Palm devices can draw a virtual keyboard and Windows CE can use symbol-recognition software for input.

Typical PDA hardware includes:

- a full colour touch-screen display;
- internal memory card extensions;

---

[5] Psion recently left the Symbian consortium (see http://www.psion.com) and switched to industrial PDAs and services.

- some limited audio and video playback capabilities and
- high-end processors (the most frequently used architecture is ARM: Intel StrongARM and XScale processors up to 600-MHz clock frequency).

Some PDAs also provide a full keyboard and a camera.

There is a wireless link using IR, Bluetooth, Wi-Fi and, in some cases, more than one of these.

Initially, both Palm and Windows CE provided limited network capability (essentially just for synchronisation with a PC) and some RPC functions in their respective SDK. They then evolved to support the full range of networks, both wired and unwired. Some customisation of the OS has been done for devices where network support is a key feature: this is where the borderline between PDA and PDA phones occurs.

3.3.1.3 PDA Phones and Smart Phones[6]

The most interesting area for wireless programmers is that of PDA phones. These are no longer simple GSM phones, which are mainly just that, phones. Today, high-end phones have huge programming capabilities and a large amount of memory installed (ranging from tens to hundreds of megabytes). Every manufacturer uses one or more proper OSs that have evolved through several generations of development. These OSs are sometimes produced by specialist companies, separate from the phone manufacturer, so that different manufacturers often share the same OS. This situation resembles that of the 1980 decade's desktop computers with many different hardware producers and a growing base of semi-independent software houses.

In this context the most important single element to be emphasised in a mobile phone is the OS since these can support, through drivers, any kind of hardware (digital cameras, extension boards on standard peripheral busses, etc.). The OS dictates, along with the software itself, the strategic concept that a company has chosen to drive development.

Proprietary OSs are usually not open to third-party programmers so that currently the most interesting OSs from a developer's perspective are in some way open:

1. *Symbian* is an evolution of the EPOC OS originally developed by Psion for its PDA. Symbian is owned and promoted by an independent British software company held by a consortium whose biggest member is Nokia. The OS is 'open' in the sense that developers can freely get source code, when they become members of

---

[6] PDA phones and smart phones are mentioned as if they were the same thing. There is a small difference since PDA phones usually look like PDAs with some added phone capabilities while smart phones emphasise the mobile phone origin. However, these differences are vanishing.

the consortium. It seems that some partners are moving out of the consortium perhaps because of technical or marketing strategies. Many high-end mobile phones already support Symbian (see http://www.symbian.com). From a programmer's perspective, Symbian is an OS with a powerful C++ like framework (some C++ features are not supported) and a flexible windowing system customisable for different devices. The greatest advantage Symbian has is that it has been developed for low-resource devices, so it addresses possible application failures due to low resources, memory leaks (very important for an OS that almost never shuts down) and similar issues.

2. *Windows Mobile* is the Microsoft effort to get into the wireless world. Microsoft tried to get a stripped down version of its flagship OS to be used with low-resource devices (PDA, see below). Later, a further customisation has been developed for mobile phones. The main advantage for developers is that this OS has much commonality with the usual Windows programming environment so it is easy for developers to adopt it (far easier compared to Symbian). However, practical performance is still questioned (it has massive hardware overheads) and, at the same time, commercial considerations such as phone manufacturers' dependencies on Redmond's corporation suggest caution.

Palm OS also is available on some mobile terminals with its programming framework. It is not clear if the OS will be available on non-Palm devices (e.g. Sony which makes some interesting Palm OS-based PDAs).

Other cross-platform OSs (that may gain momentum in the future) are some stripped down version of the open-source Linux, which would have similar advantages to Windows Mobile without the disadvantage of the proprietary link.

An interesting approach has been taken in SavaJe OS [8] which is a full Java OS that is fully Java based. It provides maximum code portability without enforcing programmers to exist in the J2ME sandbox [15–16]. However, it is not clear if it has a real chance in the market or not.

Smart phones' hardware is derived from both PDA and mobile phones. Sometimes smart phones have two processors, one dedicated to telephony and the other to applications (ARM-based CPUs are widely deployed).

It is interesting to observe input management: the problem is that PDAs, which have the greatest flexibility for input (touch screen, writing recognition, and keyboards), are not easy to use as one-hand devices as phones usually are. At the same time, input keypads are not flexible enough for generic data management use. Adopted solutions range from full to small-size keyboards, to touch screens, to a mix of both keypads and touch screen. This last one seems to be the most flexible approach because it provides both the usual phone keypad and a full touch screen (or keyboard).

As for PDAs, smart phones can be extended with external memory cards and some provide navigation support (which requires more computing power), linked with GPS. Network assistance for localisation (A-GPS) can be very useful, and some UMTS phones already provide it.

As the network bandwidth grows with UMTS, video communication has become available so that an internal camera is now a necessary feature for this class of devices.

3.3.1.4 Others

Remember that a wireless link can be used just as another kind of connection for computers. Among them, notebooks and tablet PCs can be considered PDAs' big brothers. They were not independently considered here because the observations made for PDAs can also be applied to those devices.

Below are various approaches that can be used in wireless programming with their relationships to the usual 'desktop' programming.

All the technologies described are intended for the three main device families described here.

3.4 Programming Technologies (Languages and Frameworks)

3.4.1 Overview

The question both managers and developers face as they start a project in the wireless field is 'Which technology should be chosen and why?' This part of the chapter tries to answer this question.

Our target developers are those without a special, privileged link with manufacturers. They must take a series of decisions, and they can find below some implementation samples, each using a publicly available approach and pointing out advantages and disadvantages.

Devices can be programmed using *thin* or *fat* clients. The server side in practice does not require any special programming (except for some WAP/WML cases).

Thin clients are chosen when the client part of the service does not require large amounts of computing power and the user of the service needs to be always connected to the network.

Fat clients are chosen when the client part of the service does require high computing capabilities. They are highly interactive and can be used when connecting on-demand, when synchronising data with a server for example.

Thin clients can be used on many more devices than fat clients.

The table below summarises advantages and disadvantages of both approaches.

Thin-client approach	Fat-client approach
+ No specific client software environment needed	+ Powerful programming capabilities
+ Low computing power requested	+ Access to low-level hardware and services
+ Support for the majority of mobile phones	− Supportable only on high-end phones
+ Widely portable applications	− Need to develop client-specific software

WAP/WML and iMode/cHTML are considered as thin-client technologies while others are fat-client technologies. J2ME, BREW (binary runtime environment for wireless) and Mophun (described later in this chapter) lie somewhere in the middle because they try to overcome some fat-client limitations whilst still maintaining high flexibility.

3.4.2 WAP/WML/WML Script

WAP stands for Wireless Application Protocol and is a standard way of displaying Internet-like content pages on wireless clients with small screens and all the other limitations of small devices.

From http://www.w3schools.com/wap, we learn:

- WAP is an application communication protocol.
- WAP is used to access services and information.
- WAP is inherited from Internet standards.
- WAP is for hand-held devices such as mobile phones.
- WAP is a protocol designed for micro browsers.
- WAP enables the creation of web applications for mobile devices.
- WAP uses the markup language WML (not HTML).

In practice, WAP has the same meaning on wireless networks as http does for wired ones. WAP is a binary protocol that ensures data compactness that is unavailable using http. In other words, WML is for WAP whereas HTML is for http. WML is based on XML1.0 so it is stricter than HTML (it is closer to xHTML); it has been developed for compactness. Web-like pages in WML are called *decks*; decks are built as a set of *cards*, each individually displayed.

WMLScript is the Javascript-like client-side scripting language that WML browsers support.

Wireless Internet	Wired Internet
WAP	HTTP
WML	HTML
WMLSript	Javascript

To make WAP work the WML page is requested and then server should provide the page data encoded in the WAP binary form. Usually WML pages are deployed on standard HTTP servers (like Apache or Microsoft IIS) and are then converted in binary form through a WAP gateway, a service provided by the wireless operator. In practice, the WAP gateway acts like a proxy that converts textual WML pages into binary form. This way wireless operators can filter content and limit the number of available WAP sites so that WAP is often called a 'walled garden'.[7]

---

[7] The 'walled garden' term has been used since some operators started WAP services by allowing just a limited set of websites to be accessed through their networks. However, both

3.4.2.1 Server Setup

To set up a WAP-enabled site, programmers first enable a standard web server to serve WML pages. This is usually achieved by adding some MIME type support for

- file extension .wml, "text/vnd.wap.wml"
- file extension .wmlc, "application/vnd.wap.wmlc"
- file extension .wmls, "text/vnd.wap.wmlscript"
- file extension .wmlsc, "application/vnd.wap.wmlscriptc"
- file extension .wbmp, "image/vnd.wap.wbmp"

where

- .wml and .wmlc files are WML pages in textual or compact form.
- .wmls and .wmlsc files are WMLScripts in textual or compact form.
- .wbmp are bmp-like images.

As stated above, it is the gateway's duty to convert textual data into binary form.

3.4.2.2 Sample

Pages (decks) are organised in cards sets: cards are displayed one at a time. The rationale is to limit the overhead of making a new request for each card. Carefully crafted WAP sites send a deck of cards that the client is likely to move to with a single request. Here is a sample of a WML deck that can be easily written in a text file:

```
<?xml version="1.0"?>
<!DOCTYPE wml PUBLIC "-//WAPFORUM//DTD WML 1.1//EN"
"http://www.wapforum.org/DTD/wml_1.1.xml">
<wml>
<card id="card1" title="Sample page 1">
<p>A WML sample from <b>WISE</b></p>
</card>
<card id="card2" title="Sample page 2">
<p>The second page of the sample.</p>
</card>
</wml>
```

Browsers allow clients to move freely among cards in a deck but inner links like <go href="#card2"/> can be provided in the program also. WML allows the building of tables, forms and, using WMLScript, interactive scripts.

3.4.2.3 Issues

There are not many WAP sites probably due to three reasons. Two are practical and can be (in theory) easily solved:

---

because of protests and because of the collapse of WAP-based usage, network operators today usually do not limit accessibility of sites.

- The above-mentioned 'walled garden' approach, where this is still used.
- The high cost of wireless data network connections compared to wired ones.

The third one, however, is the fact that, despite marketing claims, WML browsers are often not fully compatible with each other. This means that decks and cards must be very carefully crafted to work with different devices. It is a similar compatibility problem one can find using Microsoft Explorer or Mozilla/Netscape on desktop PCs but extended to tens of different proprietary browsers. This leads to a programming nightmare except for very basic decks.

So, unless you have some specific target device in mind, it is hard to build a good-looking WAP site.

3.4.3 iMode/cHTML

iMode is the full-colour, always-on, packet-switched, Internet service for cellular phones [13] offered by NTT DoCoMo (Nippon Telephone and Telegraph DoCoMo–*doco mo* means 'anyplace you go' in Japanese and the acronym stands for 'Do communication over the mobile network'.). As the name implies, iMode was born in Japan where it is a huge success. Today, some network operators are trying to import it in Europe.

As for WAP/WML iMode is the application level protocol while cHTML (compact HTML) is the markup language used.

Unlike WML, cHTML is a subset of HTML that leaves out coding for JPEG images, tables, image maps, multiple character fonts and styles, background colour or images, frames and cascading style sheets. They are excluded due to the low bandwidth and limited screen-size of cellphones. Not only is cHTML simpler than WML for WAP phones but developers need only make one version of the site for all iMode devices, whereas WAP developers complain they must develop multiple versions for different WAP phones. Some extensions to HTML are provided, too, some symbols that can be inserted using special characters (e.g., hexadecimal value of F89F means bright sun, just like emoticons in chat programs) and some telephone specific tags (e.g. `<A href="tel:telephone number" telbook="name" email="e-mail address">`).

Another important feature that iMode has introduced is the capability to support Java; iMode devices support a specific version of J2ME [9].

iMode is still evolving and new iMode FOMA terminals (FOMA is the UMTS-like standard used in Japan) now also support videos (with usual <a> tags).

3.4.3.1 Sample

An i-Mode sample is really an almost standard HTML page. There is no need for a customised server setup but clients should have been configured correctly to use the i-Mode server.

So, a very basic sample can look like this:

```
<!DOCTYPE HTML PUBLIC "-//W3C//DTD Compact HTML 1.0 Draft//
EN">
<html>
<head>
<title>Hello</title>
<META http-equiv="Content-Type" content="text/html">
</head>
<body>
<center><img src="WISE_logo.gif" width="96" height="15"
border="0"></center>
<br>
Hello i-Mode!
<br>
<a href="tel:3335864021">Call Me!</a>
</body>
</html>
```

Note that GIF files are the only images supported by iMode devices. Also note how the 'tel:' tag is used.

3.4.3.2 Issues

iMode, unlike WAP, is a proprietary protocol which is owned by NTT DoCoMo. it needs a gateway to convert cHTML data into packets (called an iMode server).

iMode has a 'semi-walled garden' approach because, while all sites are available to customers, a limited official set (with agreements with the network operator) does not need to be retrieved through the Internet since it is directly linked to the iMode server greatly speeding up content download.

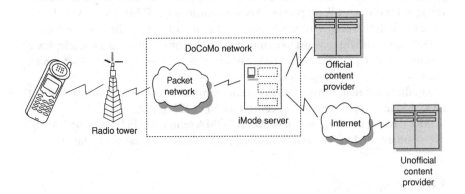

cHTML is very much easier for developers to deploy than WML. To solve compatibility issues between devices, NTT DoCoMo polices phones to ensure interworking. However, three successive versions of cHTML have been standardised (cHTML 1.0, 2.0 and 3.0) so that different devices support an increasing subset of HTML tags. Developers should code their page looking at HTTP_USER_AGENT tags (e.g. DoCoMo/1.0/F501i) to enable or disable certain features (in the sample the device is a F501i which is compatible with cHTML 1.0).

There is no scripting language in iMode, which requires more network transmission (for example, for data validation). This way, however, there are fewer requirements on the client. On the other side, iAppli (Java applications) support is enabled by default see below and [13].

3.4.3.3 Future

The wireless world is evolving and thin clients are likely to change fastest. There is evidence that the trend is for WAP and iMode to hybridise and move to xHTML, but it is still not clear if both protocols will survive or not.

3.4.4 Java (J2ME)

The Java technology achieved success in server-side applications especially as it was initially created for TV set-top boxes and embedded devices. For many years, Java was not able to survive there, primarily because of excessive hardware requirements. While moving into the server world however, continuous efforts were made to enhance Java performance (mainly at the virtual machine level) while stripping down standard packages. The first results of this effort were the PersonalJava and JavaCard specifications, made, respectively, for embedded devices and high-end smart cards. Despite some implementations, they did not succeeded in the task until Sun Microsystems decided to fully reorganise the low-end Java distribution.

There is now an entire family of Java standards defined with different packages supporting and targeting specific device classes. The picture below (taken from Sun's Java official website) describes the new whole Java family, with emphasis on the Java Micro Edition.

Looking at the picture:

1. The Java Micro Edition is split into two different sub-areas which are based on two different VMs: a standard JVM and a smaller KVM [14–16].
2. Around them are the so-called 'configurations': CDC (connected device configuration) and CLDC (connected limited device configuration). In practice, a configuration together with the underlying VM identifies a set of devices.
3. On top of configurations are 'profiles' that, in practice, are the standard packages available for the device class.
4. Above the required packages, other libraries can (or shall, in the case of Personal Basis Profile) be available.

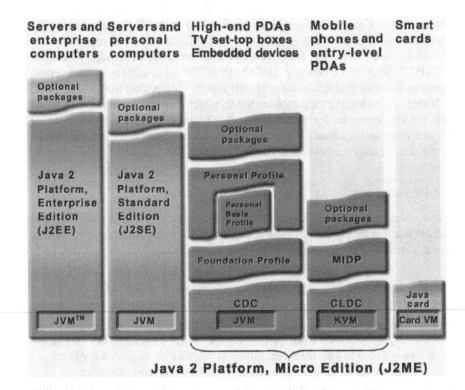

Java 2 Platform, Micro Edition (J2ME)

3.4.5 KVM/CLDC

3.4.5.1 Description

The most successful implementation of a J2ME solution is the combination KVM/CLDC (so much so that often people talking of J2ME really mean KVM/CLDC) implemented for mobile phones. To understand why, it is better to look closer at KVM/CLDC.

Quoting from [15]:

The general goal for a Java VM supporting CLDC is to be as compliant with the *Java Virtual Machine Specification* as is possible within strict memory constraints. Except for the following differences, a Java VM supporting CLDC shall be compatible with the Java VM as specified in the book, '*The Java Virtual Machine Specification (Java Series)*' by Tim Lindholm and Frank Yellin. (Addison-Wesley, 1996, ISBN 0-201-63452-X):

- no support for floating point data types (`float` and `double`);
- no support for the Java Native Interface (JNI);
- no user-defined, Java-level class loaders;
- no reflection features;
- no support for thread groups or daemon threads;
- no support for finalisation of class instances;

- no weak references and
- limitations on error handling.

Apart from floating point support, which has been omitted primarily because the majority of the CLDC target devices do not have hardware support for floating point arithmetic, the features above have been eliminated either because of strict memory limitations, or because of potential security concerns in the absence of the full J2SE security model.

Another important difference from standard Java implementation is that Java files for KVM/CLDC must be pre-verified before deployment since the VM is able to identify and reject invalid class files. Since the standard class-file verification is very memory consuming, a stack map is created at compilation-time. This stack map is then saved as an attribute in the file and, *while increasing the size of the code by about 5%, it allows KVM to verify the class code more quickly and with substantially less VM code and dynamic RAM consumption than the standard Java VM verification step with the same level of security* [15].

Java packages available in the MIDP Profile are a subset of the Java Standard Edition plus some specific packages for using a visual package (there is no java.awt in the Micro Edition) optimised for mobile phones and with a new networking package providing the so-called general connection framework. This framework can be used to support any network protocol (MIDP enforce only HTTP implementation but often other, such as TCP and UDP are available).

3.4.5.2 Sample

Below is a minimum sample application to be deployed in a J2ME KVM/CLDC device (as a mobile phone):

```
import javax.microedition.midlet.*;
import javax.microedition.lcdui.*;
public class Samplet extends MIDlet implements Command-
Listener {
   private Command exitCmd;
   private Command helpCmd;
   private Display display;

   public FirstMIDlet() {
      display = Display.getDisplay(this);
      exitCmd = new Command("Exit", Command.SCREEN, 1);
      helpCmd = new Command("Info",Command.SCREEN, 2);
   }

   public void startApp() {
      TextBox t = new TextBox("MIDP Sample", "Sample MIDP
                         app", 256, 0);
         t.addCommand(exitCmd);
         t.addCommand(helpCmd);
         t.setCommandListener(this);
```

```
        display.setCurrent(t);
    }

  public void pauseApp() { }

  public void destroyApp(boolean unconditional) { }

  public void commandAction(Command c, Displayable s) {
    if (c == exitCommand) {
      destroyApp(false);
      notifyDestroyed();
    }
  }
}
```

For a complete MIDP reference, the reference point is the Java Sun site (http://java.sun.com/j2me), but here some observations are in order:

- A MIDP application (usually called MIDlet) does not start with the usual main method but with a class extending the *javax.microedition.midlet.MIDlet* abstract class. It then implements some abstract method: *startApp()*, which is called every time the application is in the foreground, *pauseApp()*, which is called when the applications goes in background and *destroyApp (...)* which is called as the application is going to be closed. This approach ensures that some basic application features are available in every application. The OS is responsible for putting the application in background (pause) when, for example, a call is received.
- For a class to be visible, it shall get the display (with the static Display.getDisplay() call) and then set into it an object of a class implementing the *Displayable* interface.
- Commands are available and are displayed depending on device capabilities.

Two different ways for painting on a MIDP device are available. The first one is based on forms and is suitable for entering values and for web-like business applications. The second one is based on the Canvas class (which also implements the Displayable interface) and allows developers to paint freely on the screen. With the first approach, while easier, the programmers cannot control the visual behaviour of the application, while, with the second, they do not have any supporting components available and they must take care of the full interaction. The second approach leads to better graphical results at the cost of a much bigger effort, especially if different devices (which usually present different screen size and colour depth) are targeted. The best choice (which can also be a mixture of the two) depends on the application.

3.4.5.3 Deployment

A special note when using the CLDC/MIDP Profile, as well as the Jar file containing the MIDlet (which could also contain a set of MIDlets), a .JAD file shall also be deployed. This is a small text file that describes the application. It is downloaded before the application itself gets downloaded and provides some useful information to the application environment (that is the OS).

A typical Jad file looks like this:

```
MIDlet-Name: Samplet
MIDlet-Version: 1.0
MIDlet-Vendor: Sun Microsystems, Inc.
MIDlet-Description: Sample midlet
MIDlet-Info-URL: http://java.sun.com/j2me/
MIDlet-Jar-URL: sample.jar
MIDlet-Jar-Size: 2084
MicroEdition-Profile: MIDP-1.0
MicroEdition-Configuration: CLDC-1.0
MIDlet-1: First Sample,, Sample1MIDlet
MIDlet-2: Second Sample,, Sample2MIDlet
```

Examining the file

- Name and version: before downloading, the environment checks whether the MIDlet still exists on the device and if it should be upgraded or not.
- URL: where the MIDlet jar file is supposed to be and from where it is supposed to be downloadable. Often if the MIDlet file is not in this position the environment does not allow the MIDlet itself to be downloaded as it assumes it is malicious code.
- Size: before downloading the jar, the environment checks whether there is enough room available on the device or not.

The same information is also available in the usual MANIFEST file inside the jar package.

3.4.5.4 Portability Considerations

The Java motto 'write once, run anywhere' is not completely true in CLDC/MIDP for two reasons. First, many profiles and configurations mean that specific code has to be written for specific devices and second, even inside the same profile, different devices require code customisation. In some areas, in fact, the Java specification is a bit lazy, for example, in thread implementation requirements and in garbage collection, so that implementations vary a lot among different devices. The result is that some code written for a device simply does not work on other devices. Even if in theory it should (more on this in Chapter 5).

DoJa: MIDP is not the only profile available on CLDC: DoCoMo did standardise a proprietary profile called DoJa and implemented it on many DoCoMo mobiles that also support iMode. Sometimes applications written for this profile are called iAppli. For additional information see [27] or [9].

3.4.6 CDC/Personal (Basis) Profile

3.4.6.1 Description

While CDC has been specified together with CLDC, it is only recently that the Personal and Personal Basis Profiles have been standardised. Prior to this, the old Personal Java specification was implemented on devices like smart phones and PDAs. Personal Profiles are an evolution of the Personal Java specification which is, in practice, Java 1.1.6 with some minor changes (essentially some classes are not supported and a few ones have been added). It does allow native code integrations through JNI and there are some important optional packages such as JavaPhone. It also provides an AWT implementation plus RMI and reflection.

The Personal Profile ports Personal Java to the Java 2 standard; most importantly it

- provides JDBC database access which allows applications to interact with databases directly on the device;
- suggests the *Xlet* application programming model which means that the applications main class should extend the *javax.microedition.xlet* class (using a paradigm similar to MIDP development). The *Xlet* paradigm is not mandatory for application development.

Personal Basis Profile is a subset of the Personal Profile, essentially leaving out some unessential classes.

3.4.6.2 Samples

A Personal Profile basic application not featuring the Xlet paradigm looks like a common Java desktop application.

An Xlet, however, recalls the classical MIDP structure (this sample works using the Personal Basis Profile):

```java
import java.awt.*;
import javax.microedition.xlet.*;

public class SampleXlet implements Xlet {
  private XletContext context;
  private Container container;
  private Sample sample;

  public void initXlet(XletContext context) { sample=new
    Sample(); }
  public void startXlet() { sample.setVisible(true); }
  public void pauseXlet() { sample.setVisible(false); }
  public void destroyXlet(boolean unconditional) {}
}

import java.awt.*;
import java.awt.event.*;
```

```
public class Sample extends Frame{
    public Sample() {}
}
```

Basically an Xlet has the same structure as a MIDlet, having split initialisation (initXlet) and start (startXlet) methods. The code above only emphasises the capability of an Xlet to use AWT.

3.4.6.3 Extensions

Since CDC supports native methods, it is much easier to provide libraries and external packages using JNI. This is probably the most important advantage of personal profiles over MIDP because it allows companies to better customise applications on devices without requiring device manufacturers' support.

3.4.7 BREW

3.4.7.1 Description

BREW [12] is a Qualcomm solution designed for mobile phones. The idea is to provide a common programming environment for developers without requiring manufacturers to share a common OS. In some ways it is similar to the J2ME solution except for the fact that, in order to address performance bottlenecks, chip-level support is provided. In practice, BREW provides a really thin OS-like layer that, in theory, allows a very portable application development process. However, today, BREW is available only for Qualcomm CDMA chipsets.

BREW APIs have evolved over time and device manufacturers can implement only a part of them. Effective application portability can face troubles; synchronisation with native OS applications can also need troubleshooting.

BREW applications follow the applet paradigm since the environment loads them: this allows BREW to fully control the software running on the device and can be useful for online software replacement/patching.

The programming language of choice for BREW is C but, on top of C, J2ME is also supported.

3.4.7.2 Sample

Below is an application skeleton (not a complete working sample) generated by the BREW plug-in for Microsoft Visual Studio 6:

```
#include "AEEModGen.h"
#include "AEEAppGen.h"
#include "AEEShell.h"
#include "helloworld.bid"

typedef struct _helloworld {
AEEApplet a;
AEEDeviceInfo DeviceInfo;
```

```
IDisplay *pIDisplay;
IShell *pIShell;
// other variables ...
} helloworld;

/* Function Prototypes */
static boolean helloworld_HandleEvent(helloworld* pMe,
AEEEvent eCode,
uint16 wParam, uint32 dwParam);
boolean helloworld_InitAppData(helloworld* pMe);
void helloworld_FreeAppData(helloworld* pMe);

/* Functions */
int AEEClsCreateInstance(AEECLSID ClsId, IShell *pIShell,
IModule *po, void **ppObj) {
  *ppObj = NULL;
  if( ClsId == AEECLSID_HELLOWORLD ) {
   if( AEEApplet_New(sizeof(helloworld), ClsId, pIShell, po,
   (IApplet**)ppObj, (AEEHANDLER)helloworld_HandleEvent,
   (PFNFREEAPPDATA)helloworld_FreeAppData) ) {
     if(helloworld_InitAppData((helloworld*)*ppObj)) {
       return(AEE_SUCCESS);
     } else {
       IAPPLET_Release((IApplet*)*ppObj);
       return EFAILED;
   }
  }
  return(EFAILED);
}

static boolean helloworld_HandleEvent(helloworld* pMe,
AEEEvent eCode,
uint16 wParam, uint32 dwParam) {
  switch (eCode) {
    case EVT_APP_START: // app started
    return(TRUE);
    case EVT_APP_STOP: // app stopped
    return(TRUE);
    case EVT_APP_SUSPEND: // app suspended
    return(TRUE);
    case EVT_APP_RESUME: // app resuming
    return(TRUE);
    case EVT_APP_MESSAGE: // message (SMS) received
    return(TRUE);
    case EVT_KEY: // key pressed
    return(TRUE);
    default: break;
  }
```

```
  return FALSE;
}

boolean helloworld_InitAppData(helloworld* pMe) {
  pMe->DeviceInfo.wStructSize = sizeof(pMe->DeviceInfo);
  ISHELL_GetDeviceInfo(pMe->a.m_pIShell,&pMe->DeviceInfo);
  pMe->pIDisplay = pMe->a.m_pIDisplay;
  pMe->pIShell = pMe->a.m_pIShell;
  return TRUE;
}

void helloworld_FreeAppData(helloworld* pMe) {
// release application resources
}
```

The structure of the program is simple: it starts with *AEEClsCreateInstance* that is responsible for registering the application and initialising data structures. The *AAEApplet_New* function initialises structures in RAM and provides callbacks to exit and event handling functions. The main application cycle is performed inside the *HandleEvent* function.

Perhaps the most important fact is that every applet data is stored inside the 'applet structure' that is passed to every function. No global or static data should ever be instantiated. This way the environment can easily control memory allocation. Standard ANSI C libraries cannot be used.

Two other file types are needed: the MIF file (generated with a dedicated tool) that collects application unique id, icons and some other application-wide information such as privileges, copyrights, dependencies, etc. As usually happens with C programs, a resource file is needed for strings (localisation) and for external data such as dialogue description, images, sounds, etc.

3.4.7.3 Perspective

It is not clear if BREW will ever be a really successful platform or not. No non-CDMA BREW-enabled phone is yet available. This means that the huge European mobile phone market is currently not reached by BREW. Even in CDMA phones, portability depends on hardware support and API implementations (choices made by manufacturers).

BREW's target is to abstract development from hardware without too much overhead to gain important cost benefits and time-to-market reduction. BREW usually coexists with native OSs so that synchronisation between native and BREW applications can lead to integration problems.

A final warning has to be issued: a non-ANSI standard C library means that portability of code from other platforms could be difficult. At the same time, the beautiful and simple architecture can really speed up code development (more on this in Chapter 4).

3.4.8 Symbian C++

3.4.8.1 Description

Symbian is an OS targeted for mobile phones: it was previously known as EPOC and was developed for Psion PDAs. As mobile phone manufacturers looked for a common OS, they created a company, called Symbian, to adapt the Psion OS to the wireless phone market. The OS is 'open' in the sense that Symbian partners share the source code. Initially, all major phone manufacturers joined but today, the main effort comes from Nokia which owns about 60% of the company.

A couple of preliminary observations: a flexible and powerful OS like Symbian needs powerful (and thus expensive) hardware so that it is suited only to high-end phones. At the same time, a fully programmable OS is much needed by companies producing customised software for the B2B market as their customers can easily afford the cost of high-end mobiles. Because of this, Symbian has initially been targeted only at business clients (the most successful Symbian phone is the Nokia Communicator, which is clearly business-oriented).

At a later time, however, high performance requirements for mobile games led Symbian developers to enhance their platform in order to support this area. Thus Symbian is now a mixed platform with some interesting games support (e.g., graphical acceleration API).

From a programmer perspective, Symbian is C++ based. However, since C++ was fully standardised only after EPOC was released, Symbian C++ is different in many ways from standard C++. The most important difference is the lack of exception handling but, since this behaviour was essential in a resource-constrained OS where many calls can easily fail at runtime (e.g., because of lack of memory), a complete set of rules has been developed to address the problem. There is a support for '*leaving*' functions (in practice, functions that can fail without ensuring they cleaned up memory) and stacks which hold pointers to every variable (developers are responsible for this) in order to allow the system to force a clean up of memory as needed. That means that applications should then be able to be closed by the system without getting into trouble (i.e., data should be always consistent). It can look strange, at first, but this behaviour is sound and practical considering that

- A Symbian device should, in theory, never be rebooted,
- The Symbian OS cannot afford expensive memory cleaning mechanisms allowed on desktop OSs,
- The user's perception of a mobile phone is not the same as that of a user of a PC. Applications do not have to be 'closed' (in practice some applications never close) and the user should have only a hazy perception of the file system, if any view at all (there is usually no need for moving files across disks).

Another issue is that a full OS for mobile phones has to be safe: phones are potentially 'always connected' devices and hold critical information (contacts, diaries, etc.). Because of this it is important to keep data private.

3.4.8.2 Symbian Platforms

An important requirement for manufacturers was to avoid making devices appear too similar to each other: the highly modularised Symbian framework allows extensive customisation. The visual appearance has been customised and, today, different Symbian devices appear very different (in other words, more graphical shells exist). This, however, leads to some portability problems.

3.4.8.3 Sample

Below is a very simple graphical application. Symbian developers strongly recommend a 'structured' development approach using the MVC (model view controller) paradigm. However, this means that a simple application (like this one) seems over engineered. The following code follows this convention:

```
// file <HelloWorld.h> //
#ifndef __HELLOWORLD_H
#define __HELLOWORLD_H
#include <coeccntx.h>
#include <eikenv.h>
#include <eikappui.h>
#include <eikapp.h>
#include <eikdoc.h>
#include <eikmenup.h>
#include <eikon.hrh>
#include <helloworld.rsg>
#include "helloworld.hrh"


class CExampleApplication : public CeikApplication {
private:
    CApaDocument* CreateDocumentL();
    TUid AppDllUid() const;
    };


class CExampleAppView : public CcoeControl {
public:
    static CExampleAppView* NewL(const TRect& aRect);
    CExampleAppView();
    ~CExampleAppView();
      void ConstructL(const TRect& aRect);

private:
    void Draw(const TRect& /*aRect*/) const;
private:
    HBufC* iExampleText;
    };


class CExampleAppUi : public CeikAppUi {
public:
```

```
     void ConstructL();
   ~CExampleAppUi();

private:
     void HandleCommandL(TInt aCommand);

private:
     CCoeControl* iAppView;
     };

class CExampleDocument : public CeikDocument {
public:
     static CExampleDocument* NewL(CEikApplication& aApp);
     CExampleDocument(CEikApplication& aApp);
     void ConstructL();
private:
     CEikAppUi* CreateAppUiL();
     };
```

In the file above the relationship among classes is essential: in the listings below it should be noticed that the framework is responsible for creating the application object,[8] which is responsible for creating the document which creates the user interface for handling views.

```
// HelloWorld_Main.cpp //
#include "HelloWorld.h"
EXPORT_C CApaApplication* NewApplication() {
     return new CExampleApplication;
     }

GLDEF_C TInt E32Dll(TDllReason) {
     return KErrNone;
     }

// HelloWorld_Application.cpp //
#include "HelloWorld.h"
const TUid KUidHelloWorld = { 0x101F6163 };
  TUid CExampleApplication::AppDllUid() const {
     return KUidHelloWorld;
     }
CApaDocument* CExampleApplication::CreateDocumentL() {
     return new (ELeave) CExampleDocument(*this);
     }

// HelloWorld_Document.cpp //
#include "HelloWorld.h"
```

---

[8] From the point of view of the system, Symbian applications are DLLs.

```
CExampleDocument::CExampleDocument(CEikApplication& aApp)
          : CEikDocument(aApp) {
     }

CEikAppUi* CExampleDocument::CreateAppUiL() {
    return new(ELeave) CExampleAppUi;
     }

// HelloWorld_UI.cpp //
#include <eikmenub.h>
#include "HelloWorld.h"
void CExampleAppUi::ConstructL() {
     BaseConstructL();
     iAppView = CExampleAppView::NewL(ClientRect());
     }

CExampleAppUi::~ CExampleAppUi() {
     delete iAppView;
     }

void CExampleAppUi::HandleCommandL(TInt aCommand) {
     switch (aCommand) {
     case EExampleItem0:
          iEikonEnv->InfoMsg(R_EXAMPLE_TEXT_ITEM0);
          break;

     case EExampleItem1:
          iEikonEnv->InfoMsg(R_EXAMPLE_TEXT_ITEM1);
          break;

     case EExampleItem2:
          iEikonEnv->InfoMsg(R_EXAMPLE_TEXT_ITEM2);
          break;
     }

// HelloWorld_AppView.cpp //
#include "HelloWorld.h"
CExampleAppView::CExampleAppView() {
     }

CExampleAppView* CExampleAppView::NewL(const TRect& aRect) {
     CExampleAppView* self = new(ELeave) CExampleAppView();
     CleanupStack::PushL(self);
     self->ConstructL(aRect);
     CleanupStack::Pop();
     return self;
     }

CExampleAppView::~ CExampleAppView() {
```

```
        delete iExampleText;
        }

void CExampleAppView::ConstructL(const TRect& aRect) {
        iExampleText = iEikonEnv-
>AllocReadResourceL(R_EXAMPLE_TEXT_ HELLO);
        CreateWindowL();
        SetRect(aRect);
        ActivateL();
        }

void CExampleAppView::Draw(const TRect& /*aRect*/) const {
        CWindowGc& gc = SystemGc();
        TRect        drawRect = Rect();
        const CFont*     fontUsed;
        gc.Clear();
        drawRect.Shrink(10,10);
        gc.DrawRect(drawRect);
        fontUsed = iEikonEnv->TitleFont();
        gc.UseFont(fontUsed);
        TInt baselineOffset=(drawRect.Height() - fontUsed-
>HeightInPixels())/2;
        gc.DrawText(*iExampleText,drawRect,baselineOffset,
CGraphicsContext::ECenter,0);
        gc.DiscardFont();
        }
```

This application needs some explanation.

The first file HelloWorld.h is the header file; in this case, a single file is shared by all classes. The *HelloWorld_Main* file is the basic Dll file called by the system. While there are two functions, only the *NewApplication* one is important whereas the other is a remnant of the old EPOC programming framework and should be left empty. The system calls it but different implementations call it at different times so it is, in practice, not very useful. An empty implementation is the best practice.

As the application starts, a new *CExampleApplication* object is created. This object, which represents the application itself, must implement at least an AppDllUid method that returns the unique id of the application (Symbian applications must have a worldwide unique id, assigned by the Symbian organisation) and a method called *CreateDocumentL* that creates the data object for the application. The final L is a common habit of Symbian methods and means that the function can *leave* (that is, throws a type of exception).

The document created this way is responsible only for creating the user interface. In this case, the environment calls a document method for creating it and this method can leave (*CreateAppUiL*). The user interface class is responsible for handling commands (through the *HandleCommandL* method, again called by the framework) and is also responsible for creating and displaying views. These are the objects that will be displayed on the screen and in this case there is only one of them.

A common Symbian feature is the second phase constructor. In practice, the view object is created but the view's standard C++ constructor must not allocate memory or call functions that can fail so that under no circumstances can the system be left without a pointer to structures to be cleaned. As soon as the object is ready, it gets pushed into the clean-up stack. This is an area that the environment is responsible for cleaning up following a major application failure. Having done this, the newly created object can allocate memory and call functions that can fail because it could now be safely removed from memory if necessary; this process is known as the second phase constructor.

3.4.8.4 Perspective

The brief description above is still very incomplete: Symbian has many features being that it is a very interesting OS. Its biggest problem, however, is that it can be considered 'difficult' considering that the developer has to still take care of many low-level issues.

Almost every Symbian device supports Java. Business-oriented devices support both Java CLDC/MIDP and Personal Java (the older Java Personal Profile). These are the languages of choice for business applications, even if performance can sometimes be an issue.

Another problem Symbian faces is that even if every manufacturer shares the same OS, many APIs (in particular graphical APIs) are specific to a class of device. This loses full application portability across Symbian devices. For more details refer to [18,19, 20, 21].

3.4.9 Palm OS

While not initially wireless enabled, Palm was one of the first very successful hardware and software manufacturers in the PDA world. Palm has the largest market share today despite Microsoft-based devices continuously increasing their market penetration.

Palm devices started communicating with an infrared connection for device-to-device and device-to-PC synchronisation. Today, they support Bluetooth and Wi-Fi with some PDA phones also available.

In a similar manner to Symbian, the Palm OS is directed at very low-resource devices. Its framework is completely C-based [24] and attention is paid to reliability and responsiveness. Until recently, hardware performance was a bottleneck for developing Palm applications, so that high-level languages like Java were not a practical solution: on Palm there was only a J2ME MIDP 1.0 implementation. Now the situation (initiated by Palm adopting the ARM architecture) is changing and new business-oriented development environments are available.

3.4.9.1 Sample

The structure of a C Palm application is rather simple: instead of a main function is a function prototyped as

```
    UInt32 PilotMain(UInt16 cmd, MemPtr cmdPBP, UInt16
launchFlags)
```

where the types are easy to guess. This function can be called many times: it is not only used for start-up but also for reactivation after background and to stop or to pass parameters to the application (e.g., with an email application new mail can be queued 'launching' the application with the email as parameter).

After the start-up phase, the application enters the main event loop which retrieves events from the system event-queue and processes them. Below is a sample (with some detailed parts omitted) of such an application:

```
UInt32 PilotMain (UInt16 cmd, void *cmdPBP,UInt16 launch-
Flags) {
    UInt16 error;
    Boolean launched;

    if (cmd == sysAppLaunchCmdNormalLaunch) {
        error = StartApplication ();
        if (error) return (error);
        FrmGotoForm (DayView);
        EventLoop ();
        StopApplication ();
    } else if (cmd == sysAppLaunchCmdGoTo) {
        launched = launchFlags & sysAppLaunchFlagNewGlobals;
        if (launched) {
            error = StartApplication ();
            if (error) return (error);
            GoToItem ((GoToParamsPtr) cmdPBP, launched);
            EventLoop ();
            StopApplication ();
        } else GoToItem ((GoToParamsPtr) cmdPBP, launched);
    return (0);
}

...

static void EventLoop (void) {
    UInt16 error;
    EventType event;
    do {
        EvtGetEvent (&event, evtWaitForever);
        PreprocessEvent (&event);
        if (! SysHandleEvent (&event))
            if (! MenuHandleEvent (NULL, &event, &error))
                if (! ApplicationHandleEvent (&event))
                    FrmDispatchEvent (&event);
    }
    while (event.eType != appStopEvent);
}
```

The sample emphasises the two main functions for an application. The *Event-Loop* starts when the application is called for the first time (*sysAppLaunchCmdNormalLaunch*) or when the system task switcher puts the application in the foreground (*sysAppLaunchCmdGoTo*). Before entering the event loop, an application usually initialises variables and finds the application-related database. (Palm OS does not have a proper file system and data are stored in a DB-like structure.)

The other function, the event loop handler, passes the event taken from the event-queue (with *EvtGetEvent*) to routines that are supposed to handle and consume it (in this case, referring to the system, the menu, the application and, finally, the input form or view). The loop runs indefinitely until it receives an *appStopEvent* event.

As for almost every C environment, there is support for dialogues and controls through resource files, which are stored here in XML files.

3.4.10 Windows CE (C, MFC, .NET) Family

3.4.10.1 Description

Terminology: Microsoft uses plenty of names for its embedded platforms including Windows CE, PocketPC, Pocket PC phone edition, Smartphone as well as the more exotic NT embedded, Windows CE .NET, etc. Every version has many peculiarities but, from a programmer's point of view, they all provide a common feeling and so changing from one platform to another is usually easy. The successful strategy Microsoft is pursuing is to allow manufacturers to easily deploy Windows CE OS on their devices by just describing, inside their Windows CE builder IDE, the hardware components and connections. The tool should then be able to produce a customised OS for the described device.

Third-party programmers, however, face different choices. Windows CE is mainly available on PDA, where it is usually called PocketPC (implying that the device has a full touch screen). Those PDAs are now available with Bluetooth, Wi-Fi and also GSM/GPRS connections. The standard programming environment is based on a C API that can be considered an extended subset of the main Windows API. At the same time, there is an adapted MFC framework and an ATL one too, for programming using C++/COM. Microsoft distributes a Visual Basic development tool and recently, a .Net compact framework has appeared which is again a small version of the current Microsoft flagship IDE product.

As it happens, when many development environment are available, the programmer's choice is driven by the ratio between development ease and speed, power in expression and final application performance. While Windows CE is a C-based OS, the choice of a C-based development provides most flexibility but is the most difficult and time-expensive to use. Visual Basic and .NET allow rapid development but suffer in runtime performance. In addition, low-level device control with those languages can be hard. The claim is made that .NET compact framework makes network services interaction (i.e., web services) easier.

Another programming environment is growing in popularity and that is Smartphone, a Windows CE optimised for mobile phones. Being less powerful than its PDA counterpart and having to handle some differences because of the main phone-oriented activities, the programming approach changes a bit. However, the common paradigm is still available.

3.4.10.2 Sample

As for every C Windows programs, the typical Hello World application is rather long. For this reason only a typical header file for it is here (for complete examples see [20]).

```
into Instep (HINSTANCE);
HWND InitInstance (HINSTANCE, LPWSTR, int);
int TermInstance( HINSTANCE, int);
int WINAPI WinMain (HINSTANCE, HINSTANCEm LPWSTR, int);
LRESULT CALLBACK MainWndProc (HWND, UINT, WPARAM, LPARAM);
LRESULT DoCreateMain (HWND, UINT, WPARAM, LPARAM);
LRESULT DoPaintMain (HWND, UINT, WPARAM, LPARAM);
LRESULT DoHibernateMain (HWND, UINT, WPARAM, LPARAM);
LRESULT DoActivateMain (HWND, UINT, WPARAM, LPARAM);
LRESULT DoDestroyMain (HWND, UINT, WPARAM, LPARAM);
```

The application entry point is the classical *WinMain* function, whose responsibility is to

- call *InitApp*, which initialises application-wide structures including a pointer to the application's main callback function, the *MainWndProc*;
- call *InitInstance*, which creates the main application window and displays it;
- proceed with the main message loop with the three: *GetMessage()*, *TranslateMessage()*, *DispatchMessage()*.

The message-dispatching loop collects messages that the *MainWndProc* will parse and passes to the appropriate functions, as the *Do...Main* defined above.

MFC, Visual Basic and .NET applications do not add anything wireless-specific.

3.4.10.3 Perspective

Microsoft battleship is simply great and it seems they are very resolved in conquering the wireless mobile market. On the other hand, they do not have a strong background in hardware development and it does not seem they want to become hardware manufacturers (but this could change). In a few years, their platform has conquered a big share of the PDA market (mainly at the expense of Palm and Psion) but the mobile wireless market is still in the hands of mobile phone manufacturers. Those manufacturers are not willing to link too strictly with Microsoft because they probably feel that, if they do, they will lose much of their freedom (and revenues). This entire long preamble is moving towards saying that the Microsoft platform is, in theory, an optimal platform allowing Windows developers to move into the wireless world without much effort. At the same time marketing reasons could hold Microsoft in a marginal position. The best source for information on Windows CE are [23] and obviously [25].

3.4.11 Mophun

Mophun was an effort made by a company sponsored by Sony Ericsson and Nokia to provide a C framework targeted at mobile phone entertainment. They observed that while interesting, J2ME (MIDP) with its semi-interpreted structure leads to performance bottlenecks that could be effectively addressed using C code. The Mophun framework is C-based and portable and it does not require the implementation of a standard VM, which can be difficult and usually requires expensive hardware. It just requires a common set of APIs on the platform. Mophun provides, too, a sandbox-like system that blocks code from accessing host devices.

Mophun's lack of success is a big issue for portability; its total orientation towards games does not attract business developers.

3.5 Cross Development

When a service needs to be developed for multiple client platforms and when the thin approach is not feasible, then it is often difficult to maintain the same code under different programming regimes. This is the common problem that Java tries to solve; write once, read many.

Another approach is that of the Appforge Crossfire tool (see [28]) that is an IDE that plugs into Microsoft's Visual Studio .NET and allows developers to write applications in Visual Basic .NET using some components they provide for Palm, PocketPC and Symbian devices.

The concept is similar to that of Java but the tool can be compared to Personal Java and it is available for devices where high-end Java solution is not available (i.e., Symbian series 60 mobile phones where only the MIDP profile is available).

This approach is interesting because it does not rely on support by manufacturers but, instead, it is the Appforge team that provides common components for every target platform. Third-party developers can extend the framework and develop native components using a JNI-like approach.

The problem is that it requires a relatively big library on the target device so that only high-end devices can host it. Hardware enhancements, however, can make this requirement easier to satisfy. It works only for open platforms since Appforge developers have no access to manufacturers' proprietary OSs.

3.6 To Sum Up

Many technologies for developing services targeted at mobile devices have been described in this chapter.

Services can be fat or thin, meaning that they can be developed either in a manner that forces clients to download and install relatively heavy applications (fat) or they can act like web pages do in the wired Internet (thin).

Some approaches try to get the flexibility provided by fat clients and the portability provided by thin services.

The technology to be chosen depends on the target user. Many possibilities are available ranging from the mass market to a fully controlled specific business client.

The choice is made harder by the fact that a decision to go with one technology commits a developer to investment for some time and so some 'political' decisions have to be taken ('Is Microsoft to be trusted?', 'Is Java really cross platform?', etc.) and they often depend on target users, too.

Finally, some further observations about the foreseeable future to be kept in mind:

1. As per Moore's law, hardware is getting faster every day. Always remember that today's performance and memory constraints can vanish overnight.
2. The vast majority of mobile hardware manufacturers are currently concentrating on ARM-based platforms, which could focus development just as the adoption of the IBM architecture did for desktop PCs.
3. Millions of new network devices will require many network addresses so it will be a common issue to handle NAT gateways and IPv6.
4. Applications are becoming applets (Dll) with many entry points. Consider this carefully when planning user interaction.
5. Device-dependent customisation is always needed as there is no real cross-platform environment and porting can be anywhere from quite easy to extremely hard.

References

1. Bluetooth: http://www.bluetooth.com
2. Bluetooth Security: http://www.niksula.cs.hut.fi/~jiitv/bluesec.html
3. Wi-Fi: http://www.wi-fi.org
4. Wi-Fi security: http://www.isaac.cs.berkeley.edu/isaac/wep-slides.pdf
5. Wi-Fi security: http://www.isaac.cs.berkeley.edu/isaac/mobicom.pdf
6. Wi-Fi security: http://www.cs.umd.edu/~waa/wireless.html
7. Wi-Fi security: http://www.cypherpunks.ca/bh2001/
8. SavaJe: http://www.savaje.com
9. i-Mode: http://www.nttdocomo.co.jp/english/p_s/imode
10. WAP: http://www.wapforum.org
11. Markup samples: http://www.w3schools.com
12. BREW: http://brew.qualcomm.com
13. i-Mode: http://www-106.ibm.com/developerworks/wireless/library/wi-imode/?open&l=803,t=grwi,p=imode
14. Lindholm, T., Yellin, F.: *VM: The Java(TM) Virtual Machine Specification*, 2nd ed., Reading, MA: Addison-Wesley (1999).

15. KVM: http://java.sun.com/products/kvm/wp/KVMwp.pdf
16. J2ME: http://java.sun.com/j2me
17. Symbian: http://www.symbian.com
18. Symbian: http://forum.nokia.com
19. Symbian: http://developers.sonyericsson.com
20. Harrison, R.: *Symbian: Symbian OS C++ for Mobile Phones*, Chichester, UK: John Wiley & Sons (2003).
21. Boling, D.: *Windows CE: Programming Microsoft Windows CE*, 2nd ed., Redmond, Washington, USA: Microsoft Press (2001).
22. Boling, D.: *Windows CE .NET: Programming Microsoft Windows Ce .Net*, 3rd ed., Redmond, Washington, USA: Microsoft Press (2003).
23. Palm: http://www.palmsource.com (extensive documentation at http://www.palmos.com/dev/support/docs/)
24. Windows CE: http://www.microsoft.com/windowsmobile
25. Java: http://java.sun.com
26. IR: http://www.irda.org
27. http://www.geocities.co.jp/SiliconValley-Cupertino/1621/ninjava/
28. http://www.appforge.com

4
Software Architecture
of Wireless Services

Jarmo Kaloja, Tuomas Ihme, Patricia Lago,
Eila Niemela, Marco Torchiano

Software architecture can be defined as the overall structure of a software system. Specifically, it defines the components of the system and their relationships [3] [21]. Architecture usually provides several perspectives on the same system to answer the varying concerns of different system stakeholders. Defining the software architecture of an application or service is a key activity in the overall design and production process. In this chapter are notations and guidelines to define the architecture of a new wireless service.

4.1 Introduction

In this chapter we describe the generic architecture of wireless systems at the conceptual level, as opposite to the concrete level that deals with the detailed design of a specific software system [12].

Conceptual level architectural descriptions help us to recognise the generic architectural characteristics shared by most wireless systems in spite of the mix of technologies used. The WISA reference architecture [14] is used in this book as an introduction to the architectures of wireless systems at a conceptual level. Such domain-specific reference architectures help to avoid having to start design of each new system from scratch and guide a designer towards standards-based and interoperable designs.

In order to bridge the gap between a conceptual architecture and a concrete system's architecture several design problems need to be solved. Patterns [5] represent typical solutions to recurring problems and are the best tools to perform this step.

In this and the following chapters the notation that is used to describe the architecture is described . Then the reference architecture for wireless services is described. Finally guidance is provided on how patterns can be used to develop typical architectures for wireless services both at the conceptual and concrete levels.

4.2 Notation

Using the methods of IEEE Standard 1471-2000 [1], the architecture of a wireless system can be shown from several perspectives which are called viewpoints. The architectural views contained in this chapter are derived from those of the conceptual abstraction level of the QADA®[1] methodology [12a], which uses four different views of an architecture, each at two abstraction levels. In this book we concentrate only on three of those viewpoints:

• Structural
• Behavioural
• Deployment

The notation used to model the architecture of wireless services is based on UML [17]. At the conceptual level of architecture design it is important to have several degrees of freedom. In fact, notations for architectural models which are too strict could limit the architect's vision. The model should be more a sketching and communication tool than a means of detailed specification. Even large modifications to the fundamental concepts of the software architecture should be easy to make.

Structural Viewpoint. This identifies structural elements and the logical relationships between them. The notation is based on UML structure diagrams, specifically the structural models which are based upon three views:

• System context as a networked structure diagram. This is a high-level form of UML deployment diagram with extensive use made of visual stereotypes that are commonly adopted.
• Domain models of information shared between conceptual entities based on UML class diagrams.
• Functional structure and relations of conceptual entities based on simplified UML class diagrams.

Behavioural Viewpoint. Identifying the dynamics of a system and the interactions among services is the task of this viewpoint. The notation for is based on UML collaboration diagrams. Special attention should be devoted to the description of collaboration between functional entities in the main use cases of the system.

Deployment Viewpoint. The deployment viewpoint is based on UML deployment diagrams and identifies the anticipated distribution needs in the system execution environment.

The viewpoints are described in detail here. Most of the sample diagrams given are taken from WISE Pilot 2 which itself is described in detail in Chapter 6.

---

[1] QADA® Registered trademark of VTT Technical Research Centre of Finland, http://virtual.vtt.fl/qada/

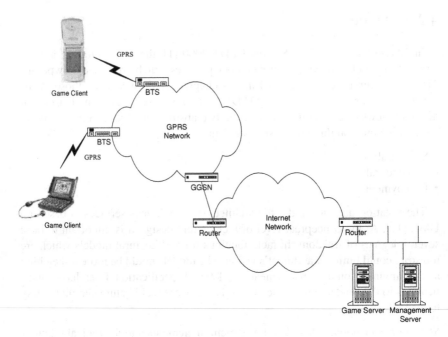

FIGURE 4.1. Example of networked structure diagram.

4.2.1 Structural Viewpoint

4.2.1.1 System Context

The system context is perceived as the description of the networked structure (Figure 4.1). Services will be positioned on top of this structure which is intended to be rather informal, aiming at showing a sketch of the environment where the system will be executed plus the hardware/software constraints already known at the conceptual level.

The networked structure diagram shows the execution environment of the system under development in terms of network resources, some nodes and the units present on nodes. In Figure 4.1 there are several network resources: the GRPS and Internet networks and the equipment to interact with them. The nodes are the user devices and the two servers, specifically, the units deployed on the nodes, are the game client and the server applications.

In general units can be acquired from external resources, e.g. software technologies or products or can represent knowledge about components to be developed.

4.2.1.2 Domain Information Models

The information models are described by using UML class diagrams. Only basic object oriented concepts should be used and implementation related concepts left

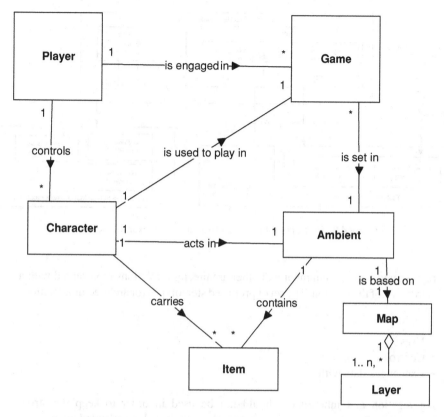

FIGURE 4.2. Example of a conceptual domain information model.

out. Inheritance and aggregation can be used but methods and attributes are usually left out or kept at a minimum detail (Figure 4.2).

4.2.1.3 Functional Structure

A functional structure is a simplified class diagram. All the architectural entities are represented as a simple classifier symbol (a rectangle). A stereotype is used to make a difference between the types of the entities (Figure 4.3). The set of proposed stereotypes for conceptual entities are:

- Domain (a set of related services, i.e. a name domain) corresponding to one of the domains defined in the reference model (see section 4.3.2).
- Application (a group of services visible to end-user)
- Service (an end-user or middleware service)

The architect does not necessarily need to consider this type of entity in the first drafts of the design because the stereotype can be added later. The composition is

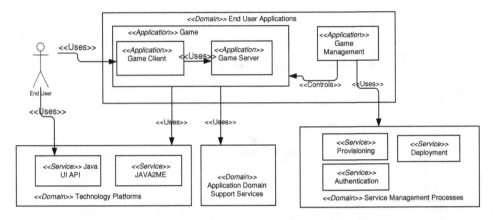

FIGURE 4.3. Conceptual functional structure of an example service.

represented with containment and other architectural relations represented with a stereotype of the relation. The set of proposed stereotypes for architectural relations are:

- Uses
- Controls
- Exchanges data with

Aggregation and inheritance should not be used in order to keep the structure clear. The structure of a conceptual entity can be presented in a separate diagram whenever needed for clarity. The structure should be presented with the minimum number of diagrams so that the overall architecture is easily visible.

The conceptual entities should be described in more detail using a separate textual description. It is preferred that lists or table formats are used for textual information instead of free form text in order to keep the structure of the architectural description clear (Table 4.1).

TABLE 4.1. Example of table format in architectural descriptions: conceptual element responsibilities

Conceptual element	Responsibilities
Game client	Provides the graphical user interface and handles the user visible subset of the game.
Game server	Handles the game status and synchronises the game state between different users.
Game management	Provides common management of a game, i.e. deploys and configures the necessary software components and provides the usage information for the billing service.

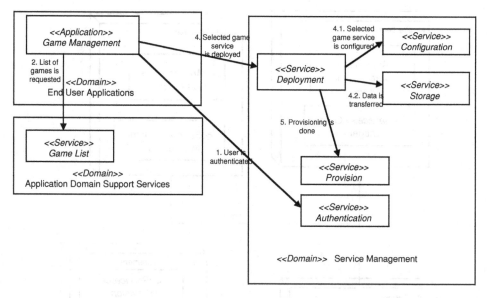

FIGURE 4.4. Conceptual collaboration in one use case of the example service.

4.2.2 Behavioural Viewpoint

4.2.2.1 Collaboration Diagram

The behavioural viewpoint is based on UML collaboration diagrams (see Figure 4.4). Its purpose is to identify the dynamics of a system and the inter-actions between services. Special attention should be devoted to the description of collaboration between functional entities involved in the main (groups of) use cases of the system. The recommended number of main use cases is around five.

4.2.3 Deployment Viewpoint

4.2.3.1 Deployment Diagram

The conceptual deployment diagram shows the conceptual structural entities as defined in section 4.2.1.3 (applications and services) on top of the execution nodes defined for the system context as defined in section 4.2.1.1. The deploy-ment diagram uses the UML deployment diagram notation. The same service can be deployed on several different nodes (as is the Game Client in Figure 4.5). In Figure 4.5, the nodes mobile terminal and game server appear along with their physical link (an http relationship). Each node also contains the functional elements defined in the functional structure diagram.

The detailed internal deployment of the services can be shown in a separate deployment diagram. This helps to analyse and describe the deployment needs for each service separately. It also keeps deployment diagrams down to a manageable

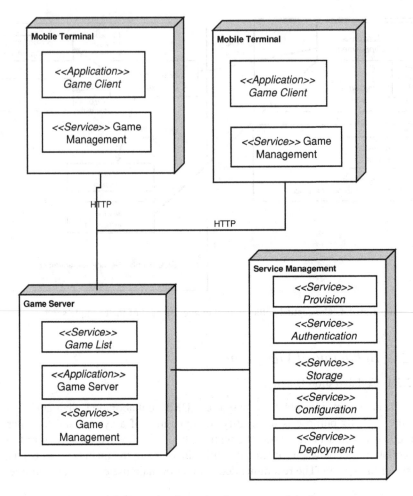

FIGURE 4.5. Example of notation for conceptual deployment.

size. The relations between entities need to be shown only when they arise from the division of a single conceptual entity into several (e.g. client and server) parts for the deployment or are considered especially important.

4.3 A Reference Architecture of Wireless Services

This section contains an overview of the reference architecture for wireless services originally described in (WISA/RA) [14]. The reference architecture of wireless Internet services defines a set of generic architectural views that help us to understand what enabling services are required from a wireless service platform, how they relate to each other, how they can be used and what is their current level of completion. This reference architecture can be used to tie together existing knowledge, standards related to wireless services, quality attributes of wireless services, applicable architectural styles and patterns and existing concepts, services and components that are considered as the driving forces in wireless service engineering.

Firstly, this section provides background information to explain the rationale behind the reference architecture in the form of an analysis of what wireless service architectures are and what kind of standards and classifications are already available. Secondly, a taxonomy of wireless services is introduced to define the division of wireless services into several domains. Several views of the reference architecture are then introduced using architectural views of which the deployment view is a new addition to the WISA/RA architecture.

4.3.1 Background

4.3.1.1 Service Oriented Architectures

The development of end-user wireless services often requires the integration of services from several development organisations. Unfortunately, as a result of this integration, there may be different layering of service logic within each individual service. As a result, services are often deployed by integrating the service logic and functionality with network elements and terminals in a proprietary and service-specific manner. Any potential for finding common enabling functionalities that could be shared by several services is not fully considered. Location-based services or service management functions are examples of such shared, reusable functions. Service architecture is the architecture of applications and middleware, i.e. the idea of service architectures is to consider not only the service as it is visible to an end-user, but also all the other enabling services needed to make that service functionality possible.

The service-oriented approach promises to help the designer maintain a better understanding of the overall service and keep the relations between service components understandable. For example (Figure 4.6) the architecture of the user interface can be kept as a consistent horizontal design problem with clear interfaces to other parts of the service architecture even when the service logic is divided between organisations. The relations between services should be kept logically clear without any technology dependencies. The service architecture is often built dynamically at runtime and the same support service may be involved in the architectures of several services for either the same or a different end-user. Consequently, the service interfaces may need to be customised at runtime for integrating the service into the architecture of a specific end-user service.

As an example, with this approach the user interface (UI) is not simply the top layer component of a service but it is made up of several components that vertically go across several layers. On top of the user interface is an enabling service to manage the application-specific user interaction for the wireless service. This service-specific UI itself can use application independent generic UI primitives. These primitives however, use one or more platform-specific APIs provided by the various wireless devices.

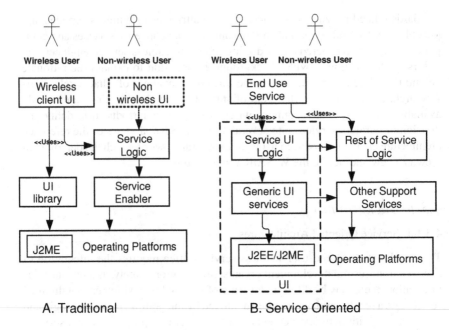

FIGURE 4.6. Visualisations of layering of software architecture.

The emergence of service-oriented architectures owes much to IP-based networking, where it is easy to create direct IP-based communication links between services and integrate the technology platforms they require using separate distribution nodes. The client side is quite standardised because of the use of browser technologies. A major benefit of service-oriented thinking in the development of wireless services could be that this kind of flexibility helps to integrate services produced by different business stakeholders and each using different technologies into a single integrated service. However, for wireless services the limited capacity of wireless links may make it more difficult to deploy services freely into separate distribution nodes. The display, keyboard, number and capacity of IP-based communication links in wireless devices are limited. A local proxy may have to be deployed into a wireless terminal for data intensive services in order to keep the communication needs over the wireless link at a minimum. This means that the various operating environments of wireless devices have to be recognised by the support service and on occasion, the required resources may not be available. Agent based platforms and dynamic customisation combined with service orientation may provide one solution for these problems.

4.3.1.2 Towards a Common Architecture for Wireless Services

Standardisation work in this field is an ongoing task and this section lists some of the most important efforts in this direction that were used as the basis of the taxonomy for the reference architecture.

The Telemanagement Forum's enhanced telecom operations map (eTOM) process model includes three vertical domains associated with the life cycle management process functions of infrastructure, product and supply chain and several horizontal layers needed for service management processes [8]. Of those the vertical domains for service life cycle management were considered relevant for structuring the service management domain of the reference architecture.

The open mobile alliance (OMA) has identified at least two classes of support services: service enablers that are used by a wireless service directly and common enablers that can also be used by wireless service enablers [16]. Several classes of enablers have been identified. Nokia has based its mobile Internet technical architecture [15] largely on this work and introduces a common platform architecture for developing future mobile Internet services. The user equipment profiles (UEProfile) defined for mobile terminals to be used by WAP services have been used as the basis of classifying technology platforms. The former UMTS Forum, now part of OMA, has defined a classification of the end-user application domain services available for third generation mobile services.

Open systems environment (OSE) [20] provides a classification of generic middleware services. The classification has been adopted by the reference architecture as the preliminary basis of further classification of generic platform services. Schmidt [19] decomposes middleware into multiple layers and describes R&D efforts related to each layer. Those layers can also be considered as a structure for commercial middleware components.

The idea behind the semantic web concept [4] is that all information is given a well defined shared meaning (semantics) by using XML, Resource description framework (RDF) and ontologies, or shared vocabularies. This ensures that different applications in the semantic web are able to communicate effectively. The software agents provide the means of exchanging the information between services. The power of the semantic web is its promise to intelligently combine information from various sources. The ontologies could provide a standard way of sharing information between services in the reference architecture, allowing the reference architecture to be used as a classification of the available ontologies.

4.3.2 An Introduction to the Reference Architecture for Wireless Services (WISA/RA)

4.3.2.1 A Taxonomy of Wireless Services

The term taxonomy may refer to either a hierarchical classification of things, or the principles underlying the classification. Mathematically, a taxonomy is a tree structure of classifications for a given set of objects.

One of the goals of the WISA reference architecture for wireless services is to help understand a wireless service from a service-oriented perspective. Another goal is to help identify the potential for both horizontal and vertical reuse of service logic and functionality and to help to define commonly usable open interfaces for the enabling services. The main dimension of the taxonomy classifies the services

TABLE 4.2. Domains of wireless services

Domain	Description
End-user services	Services visible as applications to end-users. A wireless service can have wireless users as well as non-wireless users for example, operators of wireless emergency services. Service management system users are omitted from the scope of this taxonomy and not considered here as end-users
Application domain support services	Services that provide generic services for a specific application domain on which end-user applications rely, but that are not usually used alone by the end-user, e.g. a game engine. The application domain can be scoped by specific knowledge required or similar business logic
Generic support services	Services that are needed by the end-user services and application support services, but are more generic and not directly related to any application domain such as a GPS location service
Technology platform services	Services related to specific technology (software or hardware) choices in either the mobile terminal or the server side (e.g. WML, web browser, mobile phone, Java)
Service management	Services that are needed to make the service available and link it to business processes. As such they usually are not directly related to the purpose of end-user applications, e.g. service downloading

according to how closely the service or enabling service is related to the end-user's mission.

The taxonomy can be enhanced [11] by adding an additional dimension that classifies the services into categories of related missions or related functionality provided by the service. This approach would be similar to those presented in the previous section 4.3.1.2.

The taxonomy of the constituents of wireless services has been divided into five domains which are described in Table 4.2.

4.3.2.2 Conceptual Functional Structure of Wireless Services

Section 3.2.1 has introduced and defined the five domains of the WISA/RA (Table 4.2). How the domains interact in term of 'uses', 'controls' and 'exchanges data' relationships and, more precisely, are provided here in the conceptual functional structure of WISA/RA (Figure 4.7).

The domains are organised in horizontal layers. Interaction between non-adjacent layers is allowed if it is required by end-user applications.

The service management services domain is shown as a vertical layer on the right of Figure 4.7. This is because its services interact with several components of the other domains in order to monitor and control the use of resources by a wireless service and its enabling services.

Application developers use application support services that are application-specific solutions, only reusable inside the particular application domain. These services are mostly provided as application frameworks that boost modifiability and reusability. Generic support services provide services shared by all wireless services including management level services, communication services and common

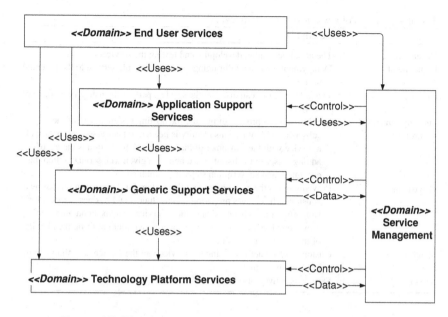

FIGURE 4.7. High-level conceptual structure of reference architecture.

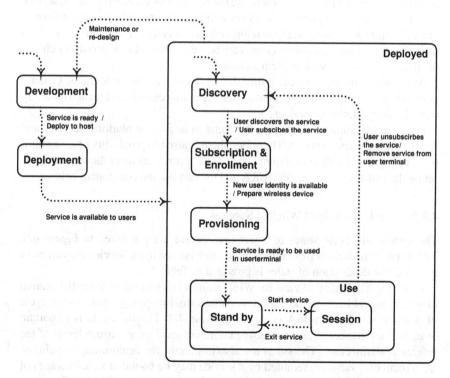

FIGURE 4.8. A state chart showing the life cycle of a wireless service.

TABLE 4.3. States of a wireless service life cycle

State	Description
Development	The act of designing, developing and testing the service
Deployment	Deployment is the act of bringing the now available service to the potential users
Discovery	The potential user can discover the service, perhaps by using a catalogue of services
Subscription and enrolment	Enrolment is the process of making the hosting system aware of the subscriber's identity. This identity is needed to later associate the use of a service with the consumer of that service. Subscription is the act of adding a user to the list of consumers of a given web service. Often the enrolment and subscription steps are combined
Provisioning	Provisioning is the act of preparing the system for the use of a service by a consumer. It involves preparing both technical and business aspects for supporting the consumers' activities. Services may be anonymous or provisioned. Anonymous services operate without requiring the identity of the consumer at run time
Stand-by	Customer is not actively using the service, but the service is available to be used at any moment
Session	Service is actively used

components for user interfaces. These are mainly used by service providers, service developers and content providers. Service management services support service providers in provisioning and managing end-user services. The relations between support services inside a domain may vary based on the end user service or choice of specific support service implementations.

Application support services utilise the services of the other domains. Generic platform services are also dependent on Service management services and naturally on technology platform services.

Potential reusability is highest in the domains of generic platform services and service management services. Therefore, there is also the possibility of using third party components if their functional and quality properties meet the requirements set by the end-user service, WISA/RA and the domain the component belongs to.

4.3.2.3 The Life Cycle of Wireless Services

The typical life cycle states of a wireless service are presented in Figure 4.8. These states are derived from information models used in the service management domain. The description of states is provided in Table 4.3.

Providing a behavioural view for WISA using a full set of detailed collaboration diagrams would become too complex. An informal mapping from the life cycle of wireless service to WISA is shown in Table 4.4. The life cycle is important to understand the collaboration between wireless services at various levels of the reference architecture. The states are also important for determining variability, i.e. a particular variation required by a service may be bound at various stages of service life cycle.

TABLE 4.4. Mapping a wireless service life cycle to the reference architecture

State	WISA/RA
Development	The WISA architectural views guide a designer to develop a service in a consistent way as part of WISA/RA
	Pattern guidelines help in implementing the service
	WISA basic services, can be used either as COTS components in design or as design examples. Some of variations between targets, etc. may be bound by the different technologies used
Deployment	The WISA service management component needs to be configured with information, such as service rating.
	A WISA deployment view shows the deployment of the WISA architecture for a typical wireless service. The actual deployment of host software is usually done at this stage
Discovery	The taxonomy helps to catalogue the services
	Support for discovery is a service of the service management domain
Subscription and enrolment	Storing the user identity is supported by the service management domain
	For some mobile services, the SIM card usually provides the customer identity
Provisioning	If the service requires software in the wireless terminal, it needs to be downloaded and initialised. The heterogeneity of wireless terminals has to be handled by, for example, different client software being downloaded. The catalogue services and design patterns provide the means to handle this
Stand-by	The application is not running in a wireless terminal
	The technology platforms may utilise this, for example the wireless connection required by the service becomes inactive to save power and avoid wasting valuable radio resources
Session	Wireless services often need to authenticate the user for each session. The service management domain provides this service. The runtime links to supporting services may have to be configured and initialised

4.3.2.4 Conceptual Deployment of a Wireless Services

The generic deployment of the WISA/RA conceptual structure (Figure 4.7) is presented in Figure 4.9 whilst details of the nodes are shown in Table 4.5.

This generic deployment shows some typical deployment units and can be customised by combining two of more units into a single unit (which requires the integration of the support services required by them). Note that this deployment is independent of the architectural styles selected for the end user service, service management services or in fact any of the services in the WISA taxonomy. For example the end user service can be deployed using client–server or p2p style. The middleware or technology platforms in the separate nodes, of the same type can differ as well. Also, for example, the service management services are often not used by the end-user directly and can be omitted from the end-user terminal or else only the monitoring/control function of terminal resources deployed.

An example of how a typical wireless service could be deployed following the above process is given here as otherwise the above reference deployment diagram may be seen as too abstract.

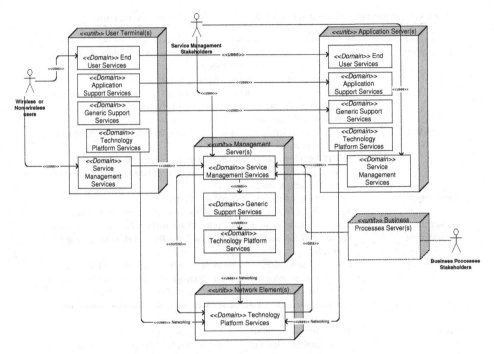

FIGURE 4.9. Conceptual deployment units of wireless services.

The example is shown in Figure 4.10. The service management functionality in the terminal node is shown as a separate service provided to the end-user. Examples of where management clients are separate from service client include SMS message based configuration of new features for the service providing easy to handle billing, or a separate management interface in a fixed (web browser based) terminal. Generic support services are often not available as identifiable services but as platform-specific implementations. The deployment units of networking and business processes are usually transparent to service developers being hidden by

TABLE 4.5. Deployment nodes of reference architecture

Deployment nodes	Description
Terminal	Wireless or non-wireless terminal used by the end-user or a terminal containing hardware control/sensor functionality. A terminal is regarded as wireless if it has no wireline communication channels
Application server	The unit containing service functionality coordinating service in several terminals
Management server	The unit containing service management functionality common to several services
Network element	The unit containing wireless or fixed networking functionality between platforms in several deployment units, such as GSM network elements
Business processes	A unit containing the functionality to link wireless services to business processes (billing etc.)

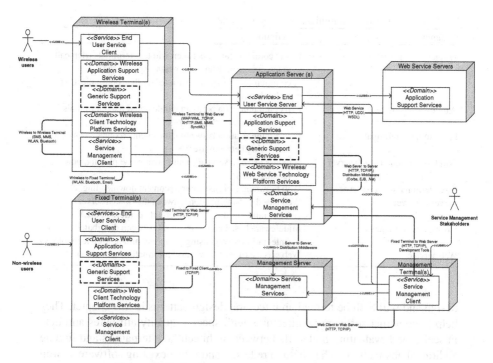

FIGURE 4.10. Typical deployment of a wireless service.

the technology platform services or management services. The choice of terminal types narrows down the possible platform choices.

The internal deployment of a service depends on the selected architectural pattern. The client–server division in Figure 4.10 should not be confused with the client–server style. Here the service client in the terminal can also contain server functionality, for example in a special case the terminal contains only a hardware or environment monitoring server. Similarly, the communication and division of service functions between terminals or application servers depends on the server side architectural style. Usually one of the application servers is a gateway for load balancing. A third party application support web service such as a content service, can be used by the application. The communication links between different types of nodes are shown in Table 4.6.

4.4 Building Typical Wireless Architectures with Patterns

Architectural patterns [5] describe the expertise of experienced developers in the fundamental overall structuring principles of software systems. Design patterns [9] describe the expertise of the developers on commonly recurring structures of communicating software components that solve general design problems within particular contexts. Both pattern categories are important in software architecture

TABLE 4.6. Types of communication links in wireless services

Communication link	Description
Wireless to wireless terminal	Direct communication between wireless terminals (rich call, voice, image transfer, text messaging etc., the communication type is restricted by the communication technology)
Wireless to fixed terminal	P2p communication between wireless and fixed terminals (content downloading etc.)
Fixed to fixed terminal	P2p communication between fixed clients (content sharing or messaging between users etc.)
Wireless terminal to web server	Wireless use of a service (multiplayer game playing, news reading, etc.)
Fixed terminal to web server	Web browsing (service control, content downloading, etc.)
Server to server	Web based communication between distributed servers (integration of different server-side platforms, etc.)
Distribution middleware	Middleware based communication between distributed servers (integration servers using compliant middleware technology)
Web service	Web service (use of third party information content, etc.)

design and will both be termed architectural design patterns in this chapter. They help to construct software architectures with specific quality attributes and help in seeing and evaluating trade-offs between architectural alternatives and finding additional abstractions. They help to redesign and refine existing software as well as to improve developer communication. The use of patterns provides a strong rationale for architectural decisions and solutions.

The adoption of patterns is a difficult process. The pattern-specific guidelines of pattern descriptions are insufficient to allow the application of patterns in building complex real-world software architectures [6, 18]. It is not always obvious which pattern to apply, because some patterns appear similar although the problem they address is different. Patterns pay attention to some specific aspects in a particular context and ignore many other important characteristics of a system. Each pattern is described in a self-contained manner independently of essential architectural aspects of the entire system. It is hard to extract relationships between patterns and derive their proper application order from their descriptions. The pattern descriptions do not address the integration of patterns into a partial design, the combination of patterns to larger design structures, the application order of a given set of patterns and the resolution of problems that cannot be solved by a single pattern in isolation [6].

Only a few patterns describe the architectural expertise of experienced wireless and mobile software developers. Few publications discuss specific examples and experiences in the adoption of trusted general-purpose patterns in the construction of mobile applications. For example, Sun's wireless blueprints contain a mobile movie ticket-ordering application (Smart Ticket) with a J2ME/MIDP wireless front end and a J2EE application server back end [23]. The Smart Ticket application showcases several important general-purpose architectural design patterns for the developers of end-to-end mobile applications.

The application of architectural styles and patterns to building real-world wireless systems is not a mechanical task. Many inter-related and competing requirements and design problems must be resolved and balanced when developing these systems. Whilst wireless software systems and traditional software systems often share similar architectural problems, the implementation context of the wireless software systems is different. The hardware and software platforms, programming environments, wireless distribution and some quality attributes of mobile terminal devices are often very specific. Some architectural patterns are used to define the overall software architecture for an entire wireless system and thus their proper ordering is not only hard, but also very important. This section discusses the selection and adoption of architectural design patterns in the construction of pattern-based typical wireless software architectures using a specific class of wireless systems as an example, specifically mobile extensions of information systems.

4.4.1 A Pattern Selection Procedure for Typical Software Architectures

Several large architectural design pattern collections are available in the literature, especially in [5, 9, 18] and in pattern databases in electronic format. These collections should be identified before starting the pattern selection process.

Very important information sources about useful architectural design patterns are the existing software architecture solutions of similar wireless systems where architectural patterns have been applied and this experience has been documented. This information can be called the domain-specific pattern information base. Many software platforms address architectural design pattern issues as well and it is necessary to take this information into account when selecting and applying patterns. This information can be called the platform-specific pattern information base.

The pattern collections in [5, 9, 18] have been created through a multi-phased evolution and evaluation process and so they can be considered as superior in overall quality, but they do not address the specific problems and implementation contexts of wireless systems. The quality of patterns and pattern descriptions in other pattern sources can vary significantly. Therefore, a specific procedure is needed for the selection of patterns for wireless systems from the different pattern sources. The selection procedure may include the following iterative stages:

1. Specify the architectural problem.
2. Identify and select patterns from the domain-specific and platform-specific pattern information bases.
3. If no satisfactory pattern-based solution is found then identify and select patterns from the collections of general-purpose patterns.
4. If no satisfactory pattern-based solution exists for the specified problem, then consider if the problem can be re-specified (stage 1).
5. If not then create a unique solution.

Stages 1, 2 and 3 will be described in detail in the following sections.

4.4.1.1 Stage 1: Specify the Architectural Problem

The architectural problem at hand must be specified precisely before trying to find a pattern that helps to solve it.

- Split the problem into sub-problems. If possible, prioritise sub-problems and try to find a pattern for each sub-problem.
- Identify the forces of the problem. The term force is used in pattern descriptions to denote any aspect of the problem that should be considered when solving it, such as the requirements, constraints and desirable properties of the solution.
- Identify associated architectural drivers. Architectural drivers enable the choice of architectural design patterns. They shape and drive the architecture of the system being built. They can be determined by analysing the purpose of the system and the critical functional, quality and business requirements. Detailed investigation of particular aspects of the requirements may be needed in order to understand their implications for the software architecture. At a more detailed level, the drivers can be determined from the requirements on the particular subsystem or component. If several pattern alternatives have to be applied for the design problem at hand, begin with the architectural driver that addresses the most important architectural aspect and the pattern that supports the driver (e.g. the limited capabilities and specific features of terminals).
- Identify the current design phase and the category of the architectural model. The architectural models of mobile extension systems are classified into two main categories: conceptual models and concrete models. The development of the concrete architectural models includes the following sub-phases: designing the system-level architecture, designing the distribution structure and designing the architecture of mobile clients and the mobile server. The models and phases do not exactly match with the design phase definitions of pattern selection procedures in pattern catalogues such as [5], which must be remembered when applying the catalogues.

4.4.1.2 Stage 2: Identify and Select Patterns from the Domain-Specific and Platform-Specific Pattern Information Bases

The second stage is to identify whether the specified problem has a pattern-based solution in the domain-specific pattern information base or in the platform-specific pattern information base. If so, then

1. Try to find the description of those patterns or corresponding pattern variants in pattern collections in the literature and pattern databases.
2. Check that the patterns have been applied properly so that the benefits, liabilities and other properties of the solution can be estimated.
3. Compare the consequences of applying the selected patterns. Investigate and compare what quality attributes the selected patterns help to achieve. Check compatibility with the platform-specific pattern information base and identify potential problems.

4. Select the pattern or patterns that provide the best solution to the specified problem. If several patterns are selected, begin with the pattern that addresses the most important aspect.

4.4.1.3 Stage 3: Identify and Select Patterns from the Collections of General-Purpose Patterns

If the domain-specific pattern information base or the platform-specific pattern information base do not provide any pattern-based solutions to the specified problem or the provided solution requires further evaluations, then try to select a pattern for the specified problem from the collections of general-purpose patterns. Note that each pattern collection tends to have specific ways to describe and classify patterns. The steps to select patterns from the collections of general-purpose patterns are:

1. Select the pattern category that corresponds to the current design activity.
   Numerous categories have been suggested for classifying software patterns with some of the most common patterns being [5, 9, 18]: analysis, architectural, design, creational, structural, behavioural and idioms. Both architectural and design categories are important in software architecture design because architectural patterns help to design coarse-grained architectures and design patterns can be used during the whole design phase.
2. Select the problem category that corresponds to the general nature of the design problem.
   Architectural design patterns have been grouped into the following problem categories [5, 18]: base-line architecture, communication, initialisation, service access and configuration, event handling, synchronisation, concurrency, from mud to structure, distributed systems, interactive systems, adaptable systems, structural decomposition, organisation of work, access control, management and resource handling.
3. Try to find the patterns and pattern variants that best match the specified problem in pattern collections in the literature and pattern databases.
   - Some collections include useful but collection-specific pattern selection procedures, such as those in [5, 9, 18].
   - Some collections additionally document the relationships between the patterns to form pattern languages, e.g. [5, 18].
   - The following sections of a pattern description particularly enable the application of the pattern selection procedure: name, intent, problem, context, forces, solution and consequences. The sections can be identified, directly or indirectly, in most of the pattern description schemata in common use today.
   - It is important to study concrete examples of architectural design patterns for applying the patterns effectively. The problem is that the examples and the Known Uses sections of patterns and pattern catalogues seldom include examples from the domain of wireless software systems. While wireless software systems and traditional software systems often share similar architectural

problems, the implementation context of the wireless software systems is different.

4. Compare the consequences of applying the selected patterns. Investigate and compare what quality attributes the selected patterns help to achieve. Some quality attributes of wireless devices may be very critical. Check the compatibility with the platform-specific pattern information base and solve potential problems.

5. Select the pattern or patterns that provide the best solution to the specified problem. If several patterns were selected, begin with the pattern that addresses the most important aspect.

If no pattern matches the specified problem, then select an alternative pattern or problem category if possible or investigate if a pattern, when refined or adapted, can help to solve the problem.

4.4.2 Applying Patterns to Conceptual Architecture

The WISA reference architecture presented earlier suggests several views of a conceptual architecture that are shared by most wireless services and, as such, are already a result of applying a number of patterns. To illustrate how to work with patterns at the conceptual architecture level, a more constrained domain is taken as an example, specifically wireless extensions to information systems.

These extensions provide a basic service to mobile phone terminal users of displaying data from information systems both graphically and textually. The quality of services is very important and a more sophisticated aim of the extensions is to strengthen the mobile presence of end users. Mobile presence aims at improving the mobile user's experience of feeling attentive, connected, integrated and focused. This can be achieved by providing the mobile terminal user with the services really needed whilst maintaining a balance between the services and the capabilities of mobile terminals and mobile communication networks.

The conceptual architecture is closer to the application domain because it is least constrained by the software and hardware platforms. Before applying patterns for designing the conceptual architecture, high-level and system-wide architectural drivers should be identified. These drivers propel and shape the conceptual architecture of the system being built. They can be determined by analysing the purpose of the system and its critical functional, quality and business requirements. Detailed investigation of particular aspects of the requirements may be needed. The most important system-wide requirements characterise interaction styles and constraints between conceptual deployment units. An example of typical system-wide architectural drivers for wireless extensions of information systems is the architectural driver 1 in section 4.4.4.

Architecture production begins with the partitioning of a system into conceptual subsystems and high-level conceptual components using the decomposition style.

The use of the pattern selection procedure for designing the typical conceptual architecture of the wireless extensions of information systems with architectural driver 1 results in the selection of the three-tier client–server style.

There are many style and pattern sources for this selection, e.g. the pearl catalogue in Chapter 5, [7], [2], [5], [13]. The tiers in our adoption of the three-tier client–server style have been selected according to [7]: the client tier, the middle tier and the data management tier. The tiers communicate in the client–server fashion.

The three-tier architecture was preferred to the two-tier architecture because of the necessity of a specific communication component between the mobile clients and the traditional information system. The three-tier architecture also has other benefits in comparison with the two-tier architecture such as exchangeability, location and migration transparency and re-configuration of servers.

The definition of the tiers in the three-tier client–server style differs between publications, see for example [13] and [7]. Furthermore, some patterns such as the client–dispatcher–server [5] are similar to the three-tier client–server style.

In the WISA reference architecture a multi-tiered architectural style is applied to the classification suggested by the wireless service taxonomy to produce a reference conceptual functional structure of wireless services.

4.4.3 Applying Patterns to System-Level Architecture

The selected and applied style for the conceptual architecture specifies fundamental overall structuring principles of concrete architecture. Producing a concrete architecture usually begins with the continuation of the system partition using the decomposition style [7]. After that the deployment style [7] is used to allocate the elements of the three-tier client–server style to the elements (nodes) of the typical system-level architecture of the wireless extensions of information systems in Figure 4.11. The client tier has been allocated to the mobile phone terminals, the middle tier to the mobile server subsystem and the data management tier to the database server system.

Similarly, the deployment view of the WISA reference architecture suggests a number of types of deployment units based on applying the decomposition style to the WISA conceptual functional structure.

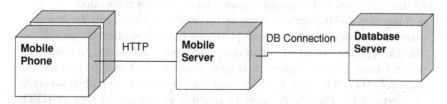

FIGURE 4.11. The typical system-level architecture of wireless extensions of information systems.

4.4.4 Typical Architectural Drivers

Many modern architecture design approaches partition software into two high-level partitions: application software and infrastructure software. The capabilities and special architectural features of the typical infrastructure software of wireless extensions of information systems, such as the software platforms and communication software strongly drive and shape the software architecture of wireless extensions of information systems. Thus, they should be considered as architectural drivers. They have also a powerful effect on the selection and application of architectural design patterns.

Architectural driver 1:

Mobile terminal devices are user interface systems that allow users to access and use application systems on demand at any time and place. They rely on powerful servers for managing several mobile terminal devices, capturing wireless-specific data from the database and managing the relational database system.

Architectural driver 2:

User interface interaction should be separated from the system's functional core.

Architectural driver 3:

Several mobile phone types are used.

Architectural driver 4:

The limited capabilities and specific features of terminals.

The Java 2 micro edition (J2ME) platform together with the mobile information device profile (MIDP) and the connected limited device configuration (CLDC), provide a complete Java runtime environment for mobile phone clients in mobile extensions of information systems (Figure 4.11). The support and structures of the J2ME platform for graphical user interfaces, threads, persistent storage and network connectivity are very important from the point of view of the application software architecture of the mobile phone clients.

The Symbian platform [10] is also often used as a platform for mobile phone clients. The platform provides the core C++ APIs and programming patterns for mobile phone designs. There are several user interfaces open to C++ programmers of Symbian phones such as Nokia series 90, Nokia series 80, Nokia series 60 and UIQ. Symbian itself provides specific conventions for processes, threads and context switching that have to be considered in the implementation of the typical software architecture.

Architectural driver 5: The limited capabilities of wireless connections.

Commercial middleware technologies for mobile environments are being researched and developed. Software platforms for mobile client devices do not include sophisticated client–server communication mechanisms. Symbian provides a more extensive protocol support than MIDP. The hypertext transfer protocol (HTTP) is often used between the clients and the mobile server as in Figure 4.11. The MIDP standard requires all devices to support HTTP. HTTP is a stateless protocol where the connection between the client and the server is terminated after each server response. A binary remote procedure call (RPC) protocol is often selected for application requests and responses over an HTTP connection. The protocol improves network efficiency because each RPC exchange can be specially designed and optimised. The self-descriptiveness of binary messages is weak and so clients and the mobile server must know the format of binary messages in advance. This means a tight coupling between the clients and the mobile server. Developers need to keep track of all code that might be affected by changes and update it when necessary.

Architectural driver 6: The features of mobile servers.

The Java enterprise edition (J2EE) platform is often used as a platform for the mobile server as in Figure 4.11. Few of the rich set of J2EE services are needed for the implementation of the basic service of wireless extensions of information systems on the mobile server. Alur et al. [2] provide a specific pattern catalogue for designing software applications for the J2EE platform.

4.4.5 Applying Patterns to Distribution Structure

The use of the pattern selection procedure for designing the distribution structure in Figure 4.12 with the architectural drivers 1, 4 and 5 results in the selection of the Broker architectural pattern [5]. The Broker pattern defines a fundamental structure for distributed software systems. Buschmann [6] provides an example on the use of the Broker pattern for designing the distribution structure of a system where multiple clients, many of which are mobile, are connected to the servers in the system.

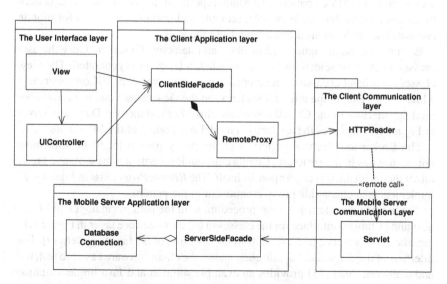

FIGURE 4.12. The typical top-level software structure of wireless extensions of information systems.

The broker component in the pattern is responsible for coordinating communication between the client and server components. The HTTPReader and Servlet classes in Figure 4.12 implement the broker component. The HTTPReader class invokes remote procedures on the server side through a binary RPC protocol over an HTTP connection.

There are some style and pattern sources for this selection, e.g. the pearls in Chapter 5, [5] and [18]. Schmidt et al. [18] provide patterns and a pattern language for concurrent and networked objects but the pattern system is too sophisticated for this system.

4.4.6 Applying Patterns to the Architecture of Mobile Clients and Servers

To successfully apply architectural design patterns to the design of the architecture of mobile terminals with the architectural drivers 4 and 5, the patterns must be selected and used judiciously. Quality attributes often conflict with each other and also with architectural drivers. For example, a set of potential patterns inspired by a set of quality attributes and architectural drivers may require a number of abstraction layers and thus probably impose too heavy a structure on simple applications that emphasise simplicity. A balance between quality attributes and architectural drivers should be achieved.

The use of the pattern selection procedure with the pattern catalogue in [5] for separating user interface interaction from the system's functional core (the architectural drivers 2 and 3) in Figure 4.12 results in the selection of the model-view-controller (MVC) pattern [5]. Many reports on the use of the MVC pattern to discover extensible, maintainable, scalable and portable structures for mobile and wireless applications are available from the web.

Each view class in Figure 4.12 displays an interactive UI screen. Once the user presses a button or selects an item from a list, a UI event is generated. The view classes event handler captures the event and passes control to the UIController class which is aware of all the interactions between the view classes and the classes behind the interface of the *ClientSideFacade* class. For instance the Database Server in Figure 4.11 includes the application model component of the MVC pattern.

The Broker architectural pattern uses the proxy pattern [5, 9] to implement remote proxies in the structure. Clients communicate with a representative proxy rather than with the server component itself. The *RemoteProxy* class in Figure 4.12 implements the client-side proxy component of the pattern.

The use of the pattern selection procedure with the pattern catalogue in [9] for designing a unified interface for the classes in the user interface layer in Figure 4.12 (architectural drivers 2 and 3) results in the selection of the facade pattern [9]. The interface of the *ClientSideFacade* class makes the client software easier to test, use and maintain. Yuan [23] provides an example solution and Java implementation of the facade pattern in the above situation.

The use of the pattern selection procedure for designing the interface between the object-oriented mobile server and the relational database management system results in the selection of the facade pattern [9]. The *ServerSideFacade* provides an object-oriented interface for accessing the relational database. The high-level interface makes the mobile server easier to test, use and maintain.

Only one facade object is required in the client and server sides. The singleton design pattern [9] helps to ensure that a class has only one instance and it can be used in designing facade classes. This provides a controlled access to the sole instance and helps to test the class.

The use of the pattern selection procedure with the pattern catalogue in [5] for constructing the software architecture with platform independence, porta-bility, exchangeability, reusability and maintainability quality attributes results in the selection of the layers pattern [5]. The Client-side software is structured into three layers in Figure 4.12: the user interface layer, the client application layer and the client communication layer. The server-side software is struc-tured into two layers, the server application layer and the server communication layer.

4.4.7 Reducing the Typical Software Architecture

The typical software architecture of wireless extensions of information systems can be reduced for simple applications. The powerful MVC pattern requires sev-eral abstraction layers and may be too heavy and too difficult to adopt by designers of simple applications. For simple J2ME and Symbian applications, the UIcon-troller class in Figure 4.12 is not always needed because controller functions can be put inside the client–side facade class, similarly the remote proxy class may be reduced from the architecture and integrated with the client–side facade class.

4.4.8 Extending the Typical Software Architecture

The typical software architecture in Figure 4.12 is open for several extensions as shown in Figure 4.13. The class names of the typical software architecture are in italics. Yuan [23] describes J2ME implementation examples of the extensions.

The client–side facade class may have a local model class for handling actions that need access to permanent data stored locally on the client device. The remote proxy class and the server-side facade class implement the same interface, the remote model interface.

User preferences may be fully cached to support personalisation. The down-loaded data can also serve as a performance cache. The remote proxy class dele-gates each requested action to a chain of handler classes, for example the cache handler class and the HTTP reader class. The chained-handler architecture is based on the request Handler interface and on the remote model request Handler abstract class.

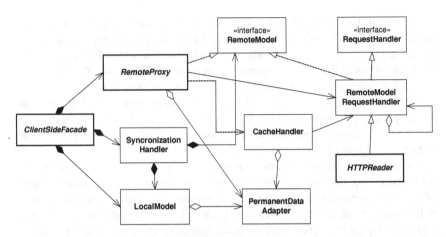

FIGURE 4.13. The typical software architecture is open for several extensions.

The synchronisation handler class synchronises data stored on the remote server with local data. The synchronisation of application caches requires complex extensions of the server side architecture (the architectural driver 6).

4.4.9 Discussion on Using Patterns

For the proposed typical software architecture, the MVC pattern was applied. This pattern [5] defines the distinctions between the model, view and controller components of the patterns clearly and cleanly. However, the MVC nomenclature in the J2ME or Symbian platform is not exactly the same as in the MVC pattern in [5]. The component boundaries of the MVC structure on the J2ME or Symbian platforms become often blurred in practice. There are two fundamental problems in applying the MVC pattern in designing mobile extensions of information systems:

- The model of MVC is split into local model classes on the client side and into model classes on the server side containing all the application logic, data and behaviour.
- The specific support and solutions of the J2ME or Symbian platforms for the MVC structure.

The overall architecture of the Smart Ticket application [23] is an example of the J2ME-specific interpretation about the MVC structure. It includes view classes, the controller class and the model layer that contains all application software.

Yuan [23] proposes that the logic of simple applications may be designed around screen classes. However, this approach may easily lead to an architecture where all classes depend on one big and complex logic class that is difficult to maintain. It is worth considering inserting the client–side facade class in this simple software structure.

Yacoub and Ammar [22] define a pattern language as 'a collection of related patterns that work together to develop a solution to an overall, usually large, problem'. Thus, the applied patterns in designing the typical software architecture of wireless extensions of information systems form an architectural pattern language. The wireless or platform-specific solutions of the Broker and MVC patterns have a potential to be described as pattern variants to be shared with the software pattern community, for example Mobile Broker, Distributed MVC, J2ME MVC or Symbian MVC.

It is possible to capture typical software architectures from existing software architecture solutions of similar wireless systems without using architectural patterns in the design rationale in any phase. However, it is difficult to both understand and use these kinds of software architectures.

The costs and risks of applying patterns in the development of software architectures of individual wireless systems from scratch are often too high. On the other hand, the reuse costs and risks of pattern-based typical software architectures can be considerably lower. Repeated use allows the amortisation of the cost of applying patterns in the development of typical software architectures for similar wireless systems.

4.5 Conclusion

The use of common notations for the architecture of wireless systems is essential for sharing and discussing the architecture between the varieties of stakeholders associated with wireless systems. This chapter has attempted to keep the selected notations and views at a minimum but still expressive enough for the intended purpose.

Only a part of the WISA reference architecture has been described here, consisting of a detailed taxonomy, a list of quality attributes, patterns usable for wireless service design and four architectural views on the conceptual level [14]. This chapter has focused on a more detailed discussion of the deployment view of the reference architecture because it provides a good overall view of typical wireless systems.

The application of patterns to the software architecture design of wireless systems is very challenging, particularly because of the specific features of the underlying hardware and software platforms of client devices and of wireless connections and protocols. The limited capabilities of devices and wireless connections require optimisation of architectural solutions.

Architectural design patterns in typical software architectures assist in constructing software architectures with specific quality attributes. They provide useful architectural principles, abstractions and communication vehicles as well as providing a powerful rationale for architectural decisions and solutions. According to experience in the WISE project, it was easy, low-risk and rapid to use those concrete structures and patterns that have been discovered to be useful and working in similar problems and platform contexts of wireless systems.

98   Jarmo Kaloja et al.

References

1. IEEE recommended practice for architectural descriptions of software-intensive systems *IEEE Computer Society IEEE* Std-1471-2000 (2000).
2. Alur D., Crupi J., Malks D., *Core J2EE Patterns: Best Practices and Design Strategies.* Upper Saddle River, NJ: Prentice Hall (2001).
3. Bass L., Clements P., Kazman R., *Software Architecture in Practice.* Reading, MA: Addison-Wesley (1998).
4. Berners-Lee T., Hendler J., Lassila O.: The semantic web. A new form of Web content that is meaningful to computers will unleash a revolution of new possibilities. *Scientific American* (2001).
5. Buschmann, F., Meunier, R., Rohnert, H., Sommerlad, P., Stal, M.: *Pattern-Oriented Software Architecture*, Volume 1: A System of Patterns. Wiley and Sons, (1996).
6. Buschmann F.: Building Software with Patterns *Proceedings of Fourth European Conference on Pattern Languages of Programming and Computing*, Bad Irsee, Germany, 8–10 July (1999).
7. Clements P., Bachmann F., Bass L., Garlan D., Ivers J., Little R., Nord R., Stafford J.: *Documenting Software Architectures, Views and Beyond.* New York: Addison-Wesley (2002).
8. Enhanced Telecom Operations Map (eTOM): The business process framework for the information and communications services industry, available at: http://www.tmforum.org/browse.asp?catIB=1647.
9. Gamma E., Helm R., Johnson R., Vlissides J.: *Design Patterns: Elements of Reusable Object-Oriented Software.* Reading, MA: Addison-Wesley (1995).
10. Harrison R.: *Symbian OS C++ for Mobile Phones.* Chicherster, England: John Wiley & Sons (2003).
11. Kalaoja J.: A step towards more efficient development of wireless services *Proceedings of the ICSSEA 2003, 16th International Conference, Software Systems Engineering and their Applications*, Paris, FR, 2–4 Dec. 2003, 2003, pp. 8.
12. Matinlassi M., Niemelä E., Dobrica L.: Quality-driven architecture design and quality analysis method: A revolutionary initiation approach to a product line architecture. VTT Technical Research Centre of Finland, Espoo, Finland, VTT Publications 456 (2002).
12a. Purhonen, A., Niemelä, E., Matinlassi, M.: Viewpoints of architectures, *Journal of Systems and Software*, Vol. 69, no 1–2, pp. 57–73 (2004).
13. Mowbray T., Malveau R.: *Software Architect Bootcamp.* Upper Saddle River, NJ: Prentice Hall (2003).
14. Niemelä E., Kaloja J., Lago P.: Towards an architectural knowledge base for wireless service engineering. *IEEE Transcactions on Software Engineering*, Vol. 31, no 5, 361–379 (2005).
15. Nokia, *MITA, Mobile Internet Technical Architecture.* IT Press (2002), available at http://europe.nokia.com/nokia/0,66864,00.html.
16. OMA: Open Mobile Alliance. At http://www.openmobilealliance.org/overview.html (2002).
17. OMG: Unified modeling language specification. version 1.5, June 1999 available at http://www.omg.org/cgi-bin/doc?formal/03-03-01.
18. Schmidt D., Stal M., Rohnert H., Buschmann F.: *Pattern-Oriented Software Architecture, Volume 2: Patterns for Concurrent and Networked Objects.* New York: John Wiley & Sons. (2000).

19. Schmidt D.: Middleware for real-time and embedded systems. *Communications of the ACM*, Vol. 45, no 6, pp. 43–48 (2002).
20. Schultz F.: Open system environment (OSE): architectural framework for information infrastructure NIST, Special Publication 500-232, December 1995.
21. Shaw M., Garlan D.: *Software Architecture, Perspectives on an Emerging Discipline.* Upper Saddle River, NJ: Prentice-Hall (1996).
22. Yacoub S., Ammar H.: *Pattern-Oriented Analysis and Design: Composing Patterns to Design Software Systems.* Reading, MA: Addison Wesley (2003).
23. Yuan M.: *Enterprise J2ME, Developng Mobile Java Applications.* Upper Saddle River, NJ: Prentice Hall (2004).

5
WISE Experience Pearls

Fabio Bella, Tuomas Ihme, Jarmo Kalaoja, Paivi Kallio, Mario Negro Ponzi, Alexis Ocampo, Aki Tikkala, Marco Torchiano

During the WISE project a large amount of knowledge was gathered. Most of it has been categorised and presented in the previous chapters. In addition there are several pragmatic little pieces of information that were found very useful in the development of wireless services.

In this chapter we present the pragmatic knowledge gathered during the project in the form of pearls. The intended use of this chapter is to provide a quick reference for ready-to-implement solutions to typical problems, either architectural, technological or process related.

The description of pearls will adopt a pattern-like format describing the applicability of patterns, the solution to the problem, citing possible additional sources of information.

First of all, we will present the format adopted to document the pearls, then we will provide an overview of the pearls, and finally we present the catalog of pearls.

5.1 Documentation Format of a Pearl

Since the pearls present solutions to recurring problems, we decided to derive our documentation format from the pattern approach [3].

The documentation format consists of seven attributes.

- **Name**: a self descriptive name for the pearl.
- **Topic**: is a list of keywords that describes the issues addressed by the pearl. The first keyword defines the type of pearl:
  - process
  - technology
  - architecture
- **Context**: describes the context of applicability of the pearl. For a process pearl it includes a characterisation of the company, the process adopted, and the project. For a technology pearl it includes a description of the system and technology.

For an architectural pearl it describes the architectural design situation in which the pearl may apply.

- **Problem**: describes the problem that is being solved by the pearl. The problem is presented in a generic form to allow the reader to select pearls of interest in a problem-oriented way.
- **Solution**: provides the solution for the problem. It includes both a structural description of the solution together with the rationale and a step by step guide for applying it.
- **Consequences**: explains which issues of the problem are solved and describes possible side effects.
- **Related information**: provides additional information. In particular, it cites known uses of the pearl in existing systems, related pearls that can be used in combination with the current one, possible variations of the pearl, and any further documentation that may be used to better understand or apply the pearl.

5.2 The Pearl System

When we consider all the pearls together with the relationships existing among them, a coherent structure emerges: we call it the pearl system.

As stated in the previous section, we distinguish between three main types of pearls: process, architecture and technology pearls. These types reflect both the origin of the pearl and, from the reader's point of view, its main application field. All pearls are listed in Table 5.1.

The process pearls provide high level tips about the organisation of the development process; they are mostly intended for project managers.

The architecture pearls lie at a lower level of abstraction and provide hints on how to structure the software; they target software architects and developers.

The technology pearls are more concrete and address problems relative to the implementation technology; they are intended for software developers.

TABLE 5.1. WISE pearls

Process	Architecture	Technology
Customer requirements gathering	Peer-to-peer (P2P)	Visual customisation
Device independent design	Reduced mark-up language	Window and UI management
Feasibility study	N-tier client–server (C/S) style	User input handling
Build test framework	Tiered style	Multiple visual layouts
	Multiple presentations	Customised deployment
	Cross-platform vs. single-platform	Low processing power
	Thin vs. fat clients	Low memory
		Network handling
		Wireless data security
		Proprietary platform
		Using emulators

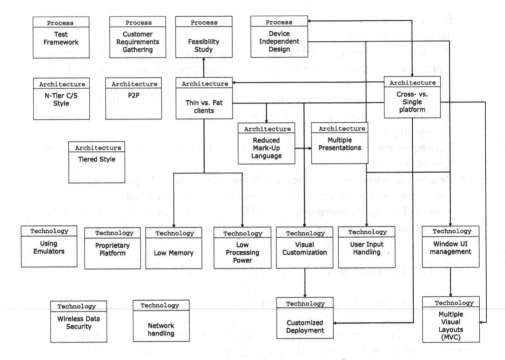

FIGURE 5.1. Relationships between pearls.

Figure 5.1 provides an overview of the relationships between pearls in the pearl system. In the figure, the pearls are represented by squares divided into two parts: the type (i.e., technology, architecture or process) is indicated in the upper part, whereas the name is located in the lower part.

Each pearl can refer to another pearl in order to implement some details of the solution or to complement it. This 'use' relationship between pearls is represented by the arrows in the figure.

For instance, a fundamental architectural decision to be taken when developing a wireless service is whether to use a fat vs. a thin client, this is the topic of the architectural pearl 'Thin vs. Fat Client'. Together with the architectural issues considered in the pearl, the 'feasibility study' process pearl can be used to decide which way to follow. When a decision has been made at the architectural level (e.g. going towards a thin-client solution), several technical problems arise, which are the focus of the related technological pearls 'Reduced Mark-Up Language' and 'Low Processing Power'.

Looking at Figure 5.1, we can observe the presence of three layers of pearls: at the top level we find the process pearls, driving the management practices; in the middle level there are the architecture pearls, driving the structuring of the service; the lower level hosts the technology pearls, driving the practical implementation decisions.

5.3 Catalogue

The rest of this chapter presents a detailed catalogue of the pearls collected during the WISE project. They are organised in reference manual style, from the higher abstraction level (process pearls) to the lower (technological pearls).

5.3.1 Process Pearls

Process pearls provide solution for problems at the project manager level.

5.3.1.1 Customer Requirements Gathering

Topic

Process, requirements process, analysis process, short time to market.

Context

Organisation with a high maturity level, incremental development life cycle process, implementation of a mobile online service.

Problem

It is difficult for developers to understand what the customer wants in a normal software project. The difficulty increases for wireless Internet services due to the lack of knowledge and experience with the business.

Solution

- The requirements should be elicited together with the customer: perform a meeting to establish what could be implemented and what should be carried out as a feasibility study. Document the results as a first draft of the requirements specification.
- Go through the customer requirements understanding the requirements, clarifying ambiguities, and identifying possible scenarios. A scenario can be represented as a UML use case diagram, or as a textual description. A scenario has roles and use cases. The scenarios are collected, split and distributed among developers.
- Specify initial requirements: the requirements specification document hosts the scenarios that are specified and formalised for the first time. Each developer is responsible for specifying a set of given scenarios.
- Review the feasibility of the user interface scenarios: before an official feasibility study, the development team checks that the user interface requirements can be developed with the actual technical support. Otherwise, the requirements draft must be changed.

Consequences

A first draft of the requirements is produced. Scenarios are derived from it and are assessed by the developers and checked by the customers. This loop enables the specification of requirements in a document that can be used to start the implementation.

Related Information

This pearl has been used for the development of Pilot 2 in the WISE project (see Chapter 6).

A possible variation of the pearl is to apply user stories. User stories are proposed by the extreme programming [1] technique as a medium to capture functional requirements in a simple, non-formal language. The developer writes them with the collaboration of the customer. The user stories are written on index cards describing the features of the system. These stories are the basis for planning iterations, tracking progress, specifying and testing the functionality. User stories seem to be suitable for requirements that change or come late in the development of the application, and therefore for wireless Internet services.

5.3.1.2 Build Test Framework

Topic

Process, testing process, short time to market, reliable testing of wireless services.

Context

Incremental development life cycle process, implementation of a mobile online service, integration testing or system testing of the implemented services.

Problem

Creating a scenario for testing wireless Internet services implies important assumptions to be made while testing the application. Different devices, different wireless networks and different user profiles must be combined to represent realistic scenarios. There are also many context factors that influence the results of the test, e.g., network traffic, user location and mobility. Setting up one suitable scenario that reflects typical user situations requires considerable effort and money.

Solution

Testing must be optimised in order to cover the service functionality at the lowest cost possible, and as completely as possible.

- Identify the hardware and software to be used: the test cases and the design's deployment view can be used to identify the system's parts.
- Set up the physical environment: connect server with clients through the required network.
- Plan the use or development of emulators/simulators: it is common for special devices or wireless networks not to be available at the moment of development. In order to avoid delays caused by waiting for physical devices, emulators/simulators could be used. However, it is important to note that emulators/

simulators do not cover all of the real device/network functionality, and therefore extra coding would have to be planned.

- Code the missing parts: test scripts could be used for configuring or executing tests automatically.
- Integrate the testing framework and perform tests to check for defects or problems.

Consequences

The risks associated with the lack of testing of wireless internet services will decrease as will the costs of performing realistic tests.

Related Information

This pearl has been used for the development of Pilot 2 in the WISE project (see Chapter 6). The developers who participated in the project performed their unit tests using emulators for WAP and J2ME. The assumption at the beginning of the project that setting up a real test of the application, i.e., the right device(s), server and network, was a complex task led to the inclusion of an activity in the process for this purpose only.

5.3.1.3 Device Independent Design

Topic

Process, short time to market, heterogeneous clients, technical problems.

Context

Organisation with a high maturity level, incremental development life cycle process, implementation of a mobile online service.

Problem

An application is device independent if it can be deployed on any mobile device keeping its functionality and capabilities. Wireless Internet services face a complex problem because of the diversity of devices on the market. It is unaffordable for software development organisations to rework their software for every new device.

Solution

Design a user interface avoiding graphical controls that can only be used by specific devices. That is, design the application thinking that it has to be suitable for both the most limited and the less limited device. Also, design for different input methods such as touch screens, keyboards and mouse.

Consequences

A device independent design is produced, which is easier to be maintained and reused.

Related Information

This pearl has been used for the development of Pilot 2 in the WISE project. Possible variations of the pearl are:

- Device independent web application framework (DIWAF). The framework is based on the single authoring principle, which consists of designing for the most capable device and automatically adapting content to different device classes. Content, layout and style are separated for reuse whenever possible.
- *XML-based approach.* The large diffusion of WML or XHTML capable browsers on mobile phones allows the design of applications that are device independent.

5.3.1.4 Feasibility Study

Topic

Process, short time to market, technical problems.

Context

Organisation with a high maturity level, incremental development life cycle process, implementation of a mobile online service.

Problem

Novelty of wireless internet technologies leads to unexpected problems that demand great effort to be solved.

Solution

Perform a feasibility study on the technical limitations (e.g. heterogeneous clients, network issues, internal and external connection requirements).
    The following steps can be applied:

- Search in the Intranet or Internet for existing knowledge about the technology and off-the-shelf products.
- Develop one or more alternative prototypes.
- Assess the technology by means of the prototype.
- Provide final conclusions in a feasibility study document; propose guidelines on how to address technical and methodological obstacles.

Consequences

The risks associated with the lack of knowledge or experience with new technologies will decrease after having researched and tried different options during the feasibility study.

Related Information

In order to refine technical requirements and decide on the technology to be used, a feasibility study was needed by Pilot 2 of the WISE project (see Chapter 6).

The feasibility study consisted of building a prototype in order to test network and mobile devices features. During the feasibility study, different communications protocols were tested to verify the data exchange rate.

5.3.2 Architecture Pearls

Architecture pearls provide solution for problems at the software engineer level.

5.3.2.1 Thin vs. Fat Clients

Topic

Architecture, clients of client server applications.

Context

Client–server application, architecture of the service, implementation of a mobile online service.

Problem

A wireless client application is 'thin' if it requires very limited computing capability, while it is 'fat' otherwise. Usually applications based on some kind of markup language (e.g. WML, cHTML) are considered 'thin' while those based on a traditional programming language (e.g. C++, Java) are considered 'fat'.

A 'thin' application has very little control over its interface. Further, it does not rely on client computing capabilities so that any non-trivial calculation has to be made on the server, thus heavily using the network link.

A 'fat' application has more control on the visual layout and it can perform computations on the client; however, it usually lacks of portability among different clients since it uses specific devices' capabilities.

Which solution is best suited for the service being built? It is very expensive to discover after the requirements phase that the choice was the wrong one.

Solution

Consider carefully the following issues to decide which type of clients to use:

- At least, three cases require a 'fat' client: applications that need a strict control on the visual layout (e.g. some games); applications that need to run also when the network link is unavailable; applications that have to perform heavy calculation on the client side.
- For other application, such as business ones, which focus on data more than on interface and heavily rely on a network link for updated information, the choice should go in the direction of a more portable 'thin' client application.
- In any case, the choice should be made within the scope of a feasibility study and consider requirements and target devices capabilities.
- If no decision can be made, opting for a 'fat' client can minimise the risks of a significant re-development since it can be easily modified to a 'thin' one.

Consequences

A careful, informed decision minimises the risk of reconsidering the service architecture in late stages of the development.

When in doubt, opting for a 'fat' client requires more effort but enables an easy downscaling of the client application as the development proceeds.

Related Information

The most successful 'thin' approach is the cHTML, used in the iMode systems. In Japan it is widely adopted for many different services, while in Europe and North America it is now growing up.

In Europe the WML, used in WAP systems, did not get the same success even if it offers almost the same capabilities and it provides a wider installed base. Common 'fat' client approaches are based on J2ME and C/C++ frameworks.

5.3.2.2 Cross-Platform vs. Single-Platform

Topic

Architecture, clients, heterogeneous clients, architectures.

Context

Selection of devices, implementation of a mobile online service.

Problem

Ideally a wireless service targets a plethora of different clients, which are based on various platforms; as a result the development of a portable service can be a daunting task.

Today, several client platforms are available on the market (see Chapter 3). They are very different and, for this reason, the realisation of a portable service is not always feasible. While there are some ongoing efforts to provide portability (J2ME and BREW among others) still many problems could arise (e.g. user interface, hardware support).

Solution

An in-depth preliminary analysis of the clients to be supported by the service is mandatory. If several different platforms must be supported, it is possible to adopt a 'thin client' solution (see pearl 'Thin vs. Fat Clients') or plan for a consistent development effort.

Otherwise, if a limited number of platforms must be supported, it is possible to select and use a suitable portable technology (e.g. J2ME, BREW; see Chapter 3). A carefully thought design (MVC pattern [3]) can also lower the development effort.

If a service is going to be developed for a single customer, it is very important to freeze the requirements about the supported platform as early as possible.

Consequences

Addressing multiple platforms requires a bigger effort with obvious cost consequences.

Using a 'thin' client approach is not always possible (see pearl 'Thin vs. Fat Clients').

Related Information

Chapter 3 is almost all about differences and similarities among clients. It must definitely be read to decide what is feasible or not with currently available clients.

5.3.2.3 Multiple Presentations

Topic

Architecture, network architecture, single point of access.

Context

User interfaces, multiple devices, multiple modalities, implementation of a mobile online service.

Problem

In a network environment, especially with wireless devices, the characteristics of client applications are often very different. It is very useful to provide the users with a single point of access to a service and automatically adapt to the client/device features.

We need to access the same service through different media and devices. As the user changes a device he/she must be offered the same service according to the device's capabilities.

In general the same service must be presented through different channels. But in practice each device has different capabilities and the details of the presentation can depend heavily on the device or client application capabilities.

This pearl provides a method to automatically detect the type of device/client and switch to the presentation mode that best suits it.

Solution

Add a presentation layer for each specific device and let it select the features that can be shown on the device and organise the contents in the most suitable way.

All the versions of the user interface are based on the same back-end component; they only adapt the information in the back-end to specific languages/devices.

In addition we need an entry point that can redirect the user to the most suitable presentation on the base of the user's device capabilities.

As an example, using Java Server Pages to provide access to devices using different languages would the structure shown in Figure 5.2.

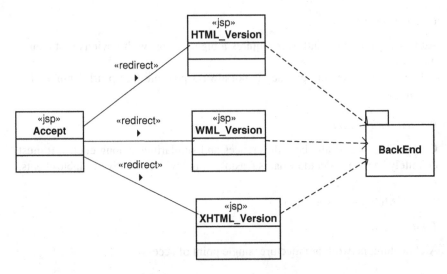

FIGURE 5.2. Multiple presentations.

The Accept JSP is the target for the connection for all the types of clients and associated browsers; it identifies the type of browser and redirects it to the version of the presentation most appropriate for that browser.

The presentation versions are thin and focus only on the presentation language and on the level of detail. The back-end component hides all the complexities and provides a unique source of information for all the channels.

Consequences

The same information is at the base of all the presentations.

Each version of the presentation is tailored for a specific device.

Each version can filter the information and provide the suitable level of detail.

As a drawback, many presentations have to be developed and maintained.

Related Information

This approach is used in several web portals to recognise the browser and use the suitable extension. This works essentially to distinguish between Netscape and Microsoft browsers.

The same approach is used to identify the type of mobile device that connects to a WAP server. This distinction is very important because the support for WML is not uniform across different devices. In this case it is possible to adapt the WML to the devices that connect to the service.

It could be used together with the MVC pattern; the *multiple presentations* pearl serves the purpose of selecting the view most appropriate for the client.

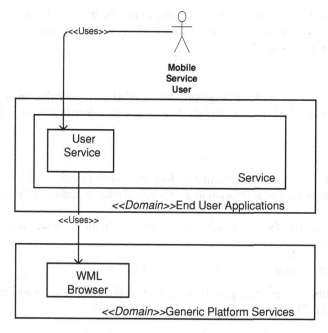

FIGURE 5.3. Functional structure of the reduced mark-up language pattern.

5.3.2.4 Reduced Mark-up Language

Topic

Architecture, presentation.

Context

User interfaces, thin-client, implementation of a mobile online service.

Problem

The problem of presenting complex structured information on a limited device can be solved using an ad-hoc mark-up language such as WML, which requires a small footprint browser.

The reduced mark-up language addresses the problem of representing fairly complex information on a device with limited capabilities. The limitations that are addressed consist essentially of

- limited display capabilities
- limited device resources usable for presentation software
- missing development effort for the implementation of an ad-hoc presentation software.

Since several recent mobile devices come in bundle with WML browsers, it is possible to leverage this built-in capability to implement all the presentation related features on the client side.

Solution

Adopt a simplified mark-up language such as WML to encode documents.

WML is standard on most mobile devices and therefore this is the solution of choice.

Consequences

It is possible to present the information formatted more or less consistently across different devices. The adaptation to the specific device is performed by the WML browser.

The browser is fairly standardised and requires reduced power and graphics capabilities.

Related Information

Several public-access web portals developed stripped-down versions for mobile phones using WML.

5.3.2.5 Peer-to-Peer (P2P)

Topic

Architecture, network architecture, decentralised division of resources.

Context

Architecture, decentralised networking.

Problem

When a high number of devices need to exchange information with each other, the presence of a centralised entity that establishes the connections can easily become a bottleneck.

Solution

P2P is used in distributed computing applications and its aim is to provide maximum flexibility. Pure P2P can be used in small wireless systems to search for information in an exhaustive way and deliver data in all file formats. Pure P2P suits well to dividing information between a limited number of users.

Nodes of the pure P2P network are peers that can act as both clients and servers. A peer has the same capability as its neighbours without a centralised router. All the nodes in a pure P2P network are equal. This differs from client–server architectures, in which some nodes are dedicated to serving the others. Each node has two routing structures: the first one is a distributed catalogue and the other is based on direct messaging.

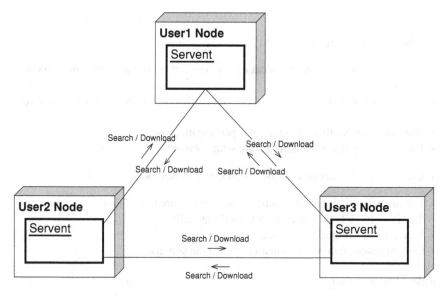

FIGURE 5.4. Deployment diagram of Gnutella.

Figure 5.4 presents the deployment structure of Gnutella, an example of a pure P2P architecture.

The functionality of Gnutella is described in the following points:

1. When you start up Gnutella, your 'servent' knows nothing of anything that has to do with gnutellaNet. This is why you have to 'add' an IP to connect to. Once your servent does connect to another servent, then they start exchanging information. Things like 'how many other servents are there and which are their IPs' are exchanged over this link. Your servent may connect to several other servents; it will communicate with all of them. Gnutella's architecture consists of dynamically changing the amount of nodes that use the TCP/IP protocol. As the connection has been established, the node uses the HTTP (Hypertext Transfer Protocol) protocol. The communication is implemented via PING messages.

2. When you want to find a file, you type in the name of the searched file. Your servent then sends it to all of the servants it is connected to, and all of them send it to all the servents they are connected to, and so on. However, each servent also searches the files it knows it is sharing and sends those results back to you.

3. Then you look through the list of files and decide to download the one you want. When you start the download, your servent tries to connect with the servent that reported the match; if it can connect it will start the download. If it cannot connect, usually because of a firewall, it will instead send a download request to all the servents it is connected to. The request will then travel the same way as the original search and eventually get to the servent that reported the match and it will try to connect back to you. This is how it is possible for Gnutella to work if one of the hosts is behind a firewall.

Consequences

P2P has the following advantages:

- The user can use resources and data from the other users and receive information from them.
- The amount of servers in the network is directly comparable with the amount of users.
- The work can be divided among the participating users.
- The users can directly communicate with each other.

The current P2P systems have the following weaknesses:

- The identities of the used resources and services are not enough transparent and they have to be localised and controlled manually.
- Search of information is limited.
- Lack of co-operation mechanism between the servers.

Related Information

Because of the weaknesses in the current P2P systems more advanced P2P architectures based on agents have been developed. When developing P2P architectures the quality and speed of the information transmitted in the network and its possible misuse has to be taken into account.

An anticipated use of P2P style involves the possibility of automotive devices to exchange traffic and road status information as they meet while going in opposite directions.

If we consider patterns described in Chapter 4, a single node in a P2P network adopts the layered architectural pattern. The functions are layered one on top of the other. The peer-to-peer system uses pipes and filters pattern to effectively transfer data from one system to another. The broker pattern is used in peer-to-peer systems. Peers access other peers or the server through the broker pattern. It acts as an interface between the system and the user.

5.3.2.6 Tiered Style

Topic

Architecture, structure

Context

A complex system that requires partitioning. Usually a system providing functionalities at different levels of abstraction, closely related to each other.

Problem

A complex software system requires to be partitioned into various parts for enhancing performance, runtime efficiency, network loading, locality of processing,

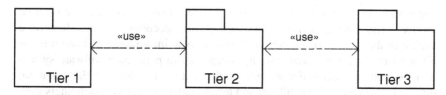

FIGURE 5.5. The tiered style.

failure recovery, functionality, modularity, manageability or scalability. The parts can be executed on different platforms or moved from platform to platform.

Solution

The tiered style is used to partition a wireless system into logically separated tiers. Each tier has a unique responsibility in the system. A tier is logically separated from other tiers in the system, and is loosely coupled with adjacent tiers.

The conceptual structure of the tiered style is shown in Figure 5.5. The use relations between the tiers can be unidirectional, bi-directional, symmetric or asymmetric.

The term tier is often confused with the layer of the layered pattern [2]; the two terms are not synonymous. Layers refer to specific layers of abstraction within an application whereas tiers refer to the physical residence of those layers (network node, process, etc.). Typically a tier hosts one or more layers.

Consequences

The advantages of the tiered style are:

- Easy to understand and manage a large software system by partitioning it into tiers with unique responsibilities.
- Support for modifiability and maintainability.

Often the tiered style is not used in isolation but closely combined with other styles and patterns, which are needed for achieving a strong impact on a software design.

Related Information

The responsibility of conceptual elements in a wireless system, data flow among elements, locality of processing, the presence and use of communication channels, and allocation to conceptual nodes of the system all tend to be presented using the tiered style.

The J2EE platform is a multi-tiered system. There are the following five tiers in the tiered model: client tier, presentation tier, business tier, integration tier, and resource tier. The client tier is responsible for user interaction, user interface presentation and client devices. The presentation tier is responsible for single sign-on, session management, content creation, format and delivery. The business tier is responsible for business logic, transactions and data services. The integration tier is responsible for resource adapters, legacy, external systems, rule engines and workflows. The resource tier is responsible for resources, data and external services. The three-tiered style has been used to decompose a mobile service system in the PALIO (personalised access to local information and services for tOurists) project. The tiered style has been used to partition a software system into the domain-specific tier, integration tier and product-line tier that point out different purposes, responsibilities and technologies as well as stakeholders such as application developers, system integrators and product-line developers.

This style is often combined with other styles such as the client–server style, the P2P style and the publisher–subscriber pattern [2], which results in a combined style such as the N-tier client–server style that shows the allocation of the components of the client–server style into conceptual tiers.

5.3.2.7 N-Tier Client–Server (C/S) Style

Topic

Architecture, structure.

Context

A system configuration is needed to be bound up with a division of functionality of services into tiers that communicate in the client–server fashion.

Problem

Within large organisation, key applications must address such issues as:

- Moving components among different platforms
- Control scalability
- Address failure recovery and reliability

When several services can evolve independently and their implementation be swapped, it is important to decouple client applications from the services they use.

Solution

The N-tier client–server architecture means an architectural style in which software functionality is decomposed into tiers that communicate in the client–server fashion. The style is a combination of the tiered style and the client–server style.

N-tier client–server structures are very often presented in architectures that combine the N-tier client–server style and the deployment style. Figure 5.6 shows a two-tier client–server architecture combined with the deployment style. In this architecture client nodes are usually user interface systems or terminals such as PCs, PDAs or mobile phones on which users run applications. Clients rely on servers for resources, such as files, devices, processing power and application and management software services. Server nodes are usually powerful computers or processes dedicated to managing disk drives (file servers), printers (print servers),

TABLE 5.2. Summary of the *N*-tier client–server style

Elements	–Component types:
	  • Clients request services of server components
	  • Servers provide services to client components
	  • Middle-tier components establish communication channels between clients and servers
	–Environmental elements: network nodes
	–Connector types: remote procedure calls, the asymmetric invocation of server's services by a client

Relations	Attachment relation –associates clients with the request role of the connector and servers with the reply role of the connector and determines which services can be requested by which clients Allocated-to relation –either static or dynamic allocation of clients and servers to environmental elements
Computational model	Clients request services from servers and wait for the results of those requests
Properties of elements	Client –Name: should suggest the functionality of the component –Type: defines general functionality, the number and types of ports and required properties –Required hardware properties –Other properties: depend on the type of the component, including quality attributes such as performance and reliability. Server –Name: should suggest the functionality of the component –Type: defines general functionality, the number and types of ports and required properties –Required hardware properties –The numbers and types of clients that can be attached –Other properties: depend on the type of the component, including quality attributes such as performance (transactions per second) and reliability. Middle tier –Name: should suggest the functionality of the component –Type: defines general functionality, the number and types of ports and required properties –Required hardware properties –The number and types of clients that can be attached –The number and types of servers that can be registered –Other properties: depend on the type of the component, including quality attributes such as performance and reliability. Environmental element –Required hardware properties such as processing, memory and capacity requirements and fault tolerance Connector –Name: should suggest the nature of interactions –Type: defines the nature of interaction (remote procedure call), the number and types of roles and required properties –Other properties: depend on the type of the connector, may include interaction protocols and quality attributes such as performance and reliability.
Topology	*N*-tiered topology: a node configuration is bound with a division of software functionality into tiers that communicate in the client–server fashion

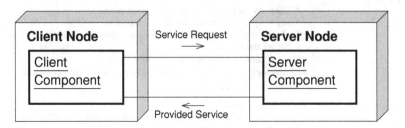

FIGURE 5.6. Two-tier client–server architecture.

network traffic (network servers) or application services. The two-tier client–server style has several benefits such as simplicity and efficiency in small systems. The style has some weaknesses such as scalability problems when the variety and number of clients and requests as well the size of the objects increase.

In the three-tier client–server architecture, a middle tier has been added between the client environment and the management server environment (Figure 5.7). This architecture provides a further separation of concerns in the overall architecture. There are a variety of ways of implementing this middle tier, such as transaction processing monitors, messaging servers and application servers. The middle tier can perform queuing, application execution, business rules execution and database staging. The three-tier architecture has several benefits in comparison with the two-tier architecture such as changeability, location and migration transparency and reconfiguration of servers.

A large variety of servers, clients and middle-tier components may coexist in the three-tier client–server architecture. The client nodes may be thin (e.g. simple web clients), rich (e.g. web clients with Java applets or ActiveX controls) or fat (e.g. distributed object clients). The three-tier architecture imposes some liabilities such as lower efficiency through indirection and explicit connection establishment as well as sensitivity to change in the interfaces of the middle-tier component.

There may be more tiers in a client–server architecture, for example, the J2EE platform is a five-tier client–server architecture including the following five tiers: client tier, presentation tier, business tier, integration tier and resource tier. Two or more of the tiers such as the presentation tier, business tier and integration tier may be allocated to one node in a distributed system.

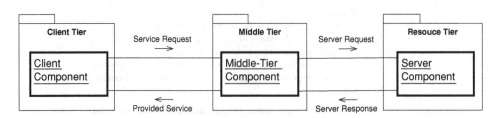

FIGURE 5.7. Three-tier client–server architecture.

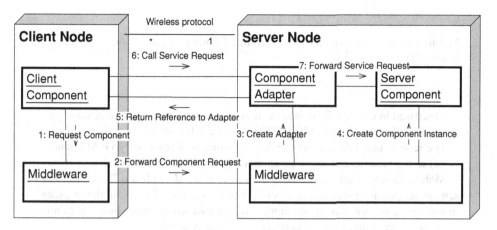

FIGURE 5.8. Middleware controls the lifetime of the component and its adapter in the three-tier client–server architecture.

Consequences

In N-tier client–server architectures, client and server components can be independently assigned to tiers or moved from platform to platform, thereby enhancing performance scalability, flexibility, failure recovery, functionality and reliability.

Related Information

N-tier client–server architectures are used in various systems throughout military and industry. The N-tier client–server style ($N > 2$) has also been applied in many wireless systems, for example to build mobile database applications using the Java technology. An example of the deployment of a three-tier client–server architecture is shown in Figure 5.8. The middle tier is implemented by the component adapter using the adapter design pattern. It has been allocated to the server node in this example. Middleware creates instances of a server component as required, and controls the lifetime of the component and its adapter. The component adapter intercepts all service requests between the client component and the server component and applies server services such as transactions and security. The client is unaware of the interception. The server component can use the component adapter, for example, for querying for client security credentials.

5.3.3 Technology Pearls

Technology pearls provide solution for problems at the programmer level.

5.3.3.1 Visual Customisation

Topic

Technology, display, screen size, GUI, content representation.

Context

Mobile devices, with small size and limited colour displays, and with limited bandwidth.

Problem

As discussed in Chapter 3, mobile devices displays are *small*. Size can vary typically from 96 × 64 pixel to 120 × 240 pixel or a little more.

The mobile network may have a *limited bandwidth* (especially GSM connections) so big pictures can also take an unacceptable time to be loaded.

Mobile devices displays *can have a limited colour depth* (even 2 colours). For screens supporting a very low number of colours (typically 2 or 4), all the graphics in order to look nice should be completely redrawn (colour reduction algorithms of graphics programmes do not produce satisfactory results).

WML and the like do not allow a satisfactory control on content representation and are just suitable to some kind of services.

Programming languages are more powerful but an application must nevertheless take in account the fact that it may be run on clients provided of very different display capabilities.

Solution

If you need to control the content representation or a customised GUI (not just a set of forms), the only solution is to use a programming language (Java/C++) instead of a mark-up language (even with scripting capabilities) such as WML.

The next hint is to use small pictures. Finally, to have better chances that your pictures are dithered in a satisfactory way on low-colour-depth devices colours, you may use contrasting colours and remark the picture edges in black (applies to logo and graphics, not to photo-realistic items of course).

When developing in Java for a PDA or PDA-like devices, the use of a windowing toolkit is highly recommended if you need to show a good looking GUI.

Consequences

Using a full-feature programming language you can achieve a better visual result requiring a longer development time.

Also, best results can be obtained only by having a per-device class customisation (i.e. a specific representation at least for each class of devices).

Related Information

The Symbian operating system, being specifically targeted at wireless devices, provides a two-layers structure: a core level that is shared among all Symbian devices and has no visual layout, and many user interface frameworks that can vary among devices (e.g. Pearl, UIQ/Quartz, etc.). As a result programmers can achieve the best results on every possible platform.

Java applications automatically achieve the platform's look-and-feel so graphics must be designed accordingly.

5.3.3.2 Window and UI Management

Topic

Technology, user interface, input devices, heterogeneous clients.

Context

Services addressing a wide range of mobile devices with different screen capabilities.

Problem

Screen sizes vary a lot among devices. A big screen can display a lot of information while a small one has to focus user attention on a single element at a time. The same service should ideally be able to display as many information as it can depending on the device it is running. This means being able to check screen size, to classify the importance of the information to be shown and to let every user reach all the information it needs in the easiest possible way.

Solution

A general purpose GUI provides several features, e.g. enabling to show, hide and move windows in a fully dynamical way. Since such features demand a lot of computing power, they are not suited for devices with limited capabilities.

It is better to study the devices the projects aims to target and group them into homogeneous categories that can share a set of customised GUI components. Engineering good user interfaces is a challenging task addressed by a broad literature. Here, two issues should be pointed out:

1. Look at the structure of the intended user interface and the information it has to present and see if it can be easily ported to different device category (e.g. does it have too much information for a small screen? Does it need some special input system, such as a touch screen?). As an example in WISE Pilot 1 (see Chapter 6) the full information about shares presented in a desktop application was not portable to a small-screen device, so a decision was taken to reduce the amount of information shown in the mobile version of the application.
2. Look at currently available 'portable' user interfaces (e.g. J2ME third party graphics toolkits), check their architecture and see if the advantages they provide are worth the costs.

The application should be able to dynamically discover the category of the device it is running on (e.g. by getting the screen size), in order to use the right GUI components.

Important note about currently available GUI libraries: except for device-specific libraries, which can obviously only be used when developing applications for a single device category, attention should be paid to general purpose graphic libraries because, as far as we have seen, they usually add much complexity without really allowing full customisation.

Consequences

In order to minimise the size of distributed code, there will probably be many distributions for each service application, depending on the client device. This should be regarded as a minor annoyance, since the majority of the distributed code will in fact be only a duplicate. A workaround is dynamically loading code through the network, but this solution can add a lot of complexity.

Related Information

This pearl is strictly tight with the user input handling one, because screen management varies also depending on device's input capabilities.

The use of the MVC pattern is recommended which will maximise code reuse.

The GUI components specific to the device category can be downloaded from a server as suggested by the 'Customised Deployment' pearl.

To manage the devices targeted by the project it is fundamental to perform a feasibility study (see pearl 'Feasibility Study').

5.3.3.3 User Input Handling

Topic

Technology, user interface, input handling

Context

Services addressing a wide range of mobile devices with different screen capabilities.

Problem

Wireless devices seldom have a full keyboard, often a keypad and sometimes a touch screen or other input systems such as voice commands. This greatly influences how data can be shown and even which data can be easily input. For example, a mobile phone keypad is thought to simplify input of numbers instead of characters while a full touch screen makes it easy to press a visual button.

The problem is to provide a consistent, usable input interface on every platform. For example, a full button-based interface can be usable for a touch screen but roughly unusable and slow using a keypad.

Solution

Group devices in categories and provide a consistent behaviour for each of them. In some cases a single category will suffice: handling a menu can be easily done both with a keypad/keyboard and with a touch screen.

Consequences

This solution poses some issues related to the deployment of the specific code. It is possible to dynamically handle such differences making applications dynamically download the right components.

Related Information

This pearl complements the 'Window and UI Management' pearl focusing on the input from the user, instead of the output.

The input components specific to the device category can be downloaded from a server as suggested by the 'Customised Deployment' pearl.

5.3.3.4 Multiple Visual Layouts

Topic

Technology, user interface, heterogeneous clients.

Context

Services addressing a wide range of mobile devices with different input capabilities.

Problem

Similarly to pearl 'User Input Handling', the problem is to handle multiple clients, each one with a possibly different level and mode of output.

Solution

As already seen in pearl 'User Input Handling', a good approach is always to group devices and develop specific clients for each group. With this approach it is very important to share code in order not to duplicate it as far as it is possible.

Another suggestion is to use the MVC pattern [3]. The MVC pattern, which is a commonly used software pattern, represents the key approach to be used when developing for heterogeneous clients.

The MVC pattern is used almost everywhere and well documented in literature [3]. Using the MVC pattern, it is possible to separate the visualisation component from the control component and the model component. Specific visualisation components can be developed for different categories of graphical devices; similarly it is possible to develop a specific control component for each category of input device.

It is worth noting that when programming on the Symbian platform this pattern is in practice enforced by the environment. Microsoft's MFC approach is a lighter version of the MVC pattern, called document view, but it is based on the same idea. Other technologies do not enforce such pattern, so designers and programmers should provide it by themselves.

Consequences

A well organised MVC application is by far easier to maintain and to port to other platforms, should requirements about supported clients change. This is particularly important because the combined technological and marketplace evolution always brings new devices, which we will probably have to support.

Related Information

The MVC is a well-known pattern; it was documented in the seminal work on patterns by Gamma et al. [3].

The MVC embedded in Symbian development environment is described in [4].

5.3.3.5 Customised Deployment

Topic

Technology, heterogeneous clients, multiple applications, deployment.

Context

Services addressing a wide range of mobile devices each requiring different components and resources.

Problem

Services developed for multiple clients lead to multiple code distributions. Also, static resources (e.g. pictures and sounds) have to be deployed on per-client basis.

It is expensive to maintain multiple distributions. A single large distribution which would include every other is most of the times simply too big for mobile clients.

Solution

Data and even parts of code can be dynamically downloaded. A small core common to all platforms should be able to identify the client group it is running on and to select the right resources to download and use. Those resources should be possibly cached for subsequent runs.

Consequences

This approach would require higher network consumption, longer time (at least for setup) and a complex architecture. It could be useful (but not necessary) if the programming language supports some kind of reflection.

This mechanism can be used for software upgrades, too. Since this is a very general purpose need, custom dedicated software could be implemented for downloading applications and resources. It could be a sort of system-level software, tightly coupled with the OS.

Related Information

See also pearls 'Visual Customisation' and 'Cross vs. Single Platform'.
Noble and Weir describe 27 patterns for small memory devices in [5].

5.3.3.6 Low Computing Power

Topic

Technology, CPU, remote computation.

Context

Services addressing a mobile device with limited computing power.

Problem

Mobile wireless devices have a small amount of CPU power compared to commonly available PCs. They are not a good choice for computing-intensive applications. Some CPU intensive applications simply cannot be handled by a mobile battery powered device. Even what we now consider not very CPU-intensive such as word processor, usually require a fast CPU and a lot of memory (e.g. for spell checking). Graphics (e.g. photo manipulations) have the same limitation.

Solution

Sometimes it is not possible to provide any workaround: a 3D action game, for example, cannot be played on a very limited device. In those situations, the only choice is to wait for hardware to evolve and, in the meantime, to develop something simpler.

Sometimes, however, especially for batch-like processing, it is possible to provide a remote interface on a server that can get all data, process them and provide feedback to the mobile client. When a small amount of data must be transmitted and the transmission time is low compared with the processing time, this is a feasible approach.

Consequences

This approach leads to higher network use and subsequent costs, latency and delays.

Related Information

Some navigation applications on the market already use this approach in order to remotely calculate trip (e.g. Wayfinder [7]).

5.3.3.7 Low Memory

Topic

Technology, memory, storage, network, remote.

Context

Mobile devices with limited memory resources.

Problem

Limited amount of memory both enforce applications not to have big local databases and not to use memory consuming algorithms (e.g. heavy recursion).

Solution

The solution to be used is the same as for the 'Low Computing Power' pearl: handle remotely requirements that cannot be satisfied locally. Also, some commercial applications, such as the already mentioned Wayfinder [7], use this approach for low resources devices.

As an example of this, in WISE Pilot 2, the game map had to be split in many parts, few stored and processed on the client, the others on the server. Storing and processing the whole game map on the client was unfeasible.

Consequences

The design of applications using this approach should carefully consider extra latency times introduced: sometimes this approach could also require some design modification.

Related Information

See the WISE Pilot 2 in Chapter 6.

Wayfinder [7] navigation application for Symbian mobile phones uses this approach.

5.3.3.8 Network Handling

Topic

Technology, network, protocols, latency, bandwidth.

Context

Services and applications using wireless networks.

Problem

Wireless link has two problems: first, it is not as reliable as a wired link and second, it is usually slower than the wired counterpart both having higher latency and smaller bandwidth.

Solution

Carefully optimise (minimise) network data transmission. The idea is to limit the bandwidth occupation of the protocol to obtain low latency.

The standard TCP/IP protocol may not meet the latency requirements. Another option is to use another protocol with lower latency, like UDP.

However, UDP is less reliable than TCP. This problem can be solved by using redundancy techniques for the subset of data that has to be reliable.

Consequences

Reliability has to be traded off for latency, and vice versa. This has to be considered in the requirements and design phases.

Related Information

WISE Pilot 2, in its first iteration, uses this pattern to cope with the limited bandwidth of GPRS network. After feasibility study (see 'Feasibility Study' pearl) TCP turned out providing an insufficient data rate, therefore, UDP was chosen as the communications protocol. Some modifications had to be made to the protocol in order to meet the device requirements.

This pearl addresses the problem deriving from the solutions in other technology pearls that usually involve high volume data transmission e.g. low memory and low computing power pearls).

5.3.3.9 Wireless Data Security

Topic

Technology, secure transmissions, encryption.

Context

Sensitive data transmitted through a wireless link. Encryption and privacy techniques and standards.

Problem

It is much easier to intercept a wireless link than a wired one since no physical hacking is needed and there are no cables to be secured. Everybody in range can easily intercept any communication. As wireless services may handle sensitive data (e.g. bank accounts, reserved remote logins, etc.) they should be able to address all relevant security issues.

Data encryption protocols usually require high computing power, so that specific algorithms have to be adopted.

Solution

Any wireless standard provides some dedicated encryption capability; WEP (wireless equivalent privacy) is adopted by IEEE802 protocols and Bluetooth also has some encryption features. Those can be considered adequate for most uses but security critical applications should implement some additional application level encryption.

Borrowing encryption protocols adopted by the wired Internet (such as https) can be unfeasible due to the limited computing power of client devices, but it is the easiest approach. Some dedicated algorithms, such as those based on elliptic curve cryptography, should also be considered.

Consequences

Encryption using protocols adopted by the wired Internet is easier to do, but expensive in terms of computing power and required resources. At the same time, dedicated algorithms are newer (and thus less tested) and not already widely adopted so that more development effort is usually needed to implement them.

Related Information

WEP, Bluetooth security, ECDSA, SSL, TLS.

5.3.3.10 Proprietary Platform

Topic

Technology, hardware, peripherals, heterogeneous clients.

Context

Mobile devices are based on different hardware. Also, the hardware can be accessed by applications in very different ways.

Problem

The access to hardware features is a critical decision. Some programming platforms simply do not allow to access hardware peripherals without an explicit support by manufacturers. At the same time, there is still no widespread adoption of standards provided for plugging additional peripherals (such as the mass storage interface adopted for desktop PC). Bluetooth is sometimes referred to as a plug-in for additional hardware and it is probably the more widespread tool adopted: almost every mobile platform with a Bluetooth support publicly provides some way to access the underlying Bluetooth link.

In general, however, accessing proprietary hardware internally built in the device is a matter of using proprietary specific libraries.

Solution

We have found no generic solution since proprietary extensions (hardware and software) are a key part of manufacturers' marketing strategies. In the requirements phase, developers should point out the hardware and hardware support that is really necessary for the application. If a Bluetooth link is available a good move could be to use the Bluetooth standard together with external hardware. For example, a positioning application could rely on external GPS receivers connected through Bluetooth thus needing only a Bluetooth support. Sometimes it is feasible to adopt the same strategy using a serial link (which is often available).

For all other uses of non-standard hardware, different distributions of the code will be needed. If possible, in any case, the best choice is to use a lowest common denominator approach, using only the hardware that is available on all target platforms.

Consequences

If more than one distribution is needed, that number will multiply by those needed as consequences of other choices (see pearls 'User Input Handling', 'Multiple Visual Layouts' and 'Customised Deployment').

If a lowest common denominator approach is used, the application not using specialised hardware will probably be considered partially incomplete.

Related Information

J2ME, Bluetooth specification.

5.3.3.11 Using Emulators

Topic

Technology, development, emulations, performance, reliability.

Context

Applications developed for mobiles are usually developed on desktop PC and tested on emulators.

Problem

Since emulators often do not emulate perfectly the wireless devices, an application running on the emulator can simply not work on the real device needing a big rework effort. At the same time, it is important not to enforce developers to test everything on real devices since such an approach would take too much time.

Solution

A good approach is to first test the emulator knowing where it is reliable and where it is not. Usually emulators have trouble in specific areas:

- Multithreading: desktop PC multithreading systems have a very reliable preemptive multithreading mechanism, which is seldom available on wireless devices;
- Network connections: the network link is that of the host running the emulator;
- Hardware peripherals: the link with them is usually wrapped through the host operating system;
- Performance: they are usually faster than real devices;
- Memory handling: they have much more memory available and they handle it more efficiently.

In general, then, unit testing can be performed on emulators but any other higher level and non-functional test should be performed on real devices. This is especially true for code parts involving the areas described above. Failing to reliably test on real devices each part of the code could lead to a huge rework effort.

Consequences

The development time for a wireless application is longer than that for a common desktop application. This is mainly due to the longer time needed for testing. Testing procedures are different from those applied for desktop applications.

Related Information

J2ME wireless toolkit [6], emulators in general.

References

1. K. Beck: *Extreme Programming Explained: Embrace Change*. Reading, MA: Addison-Wesley (2000).
2. Buschmann, Meunier, Rohnert, Sommerland, Stal: *Pattern-Oriented Software Architecture*: New York: John Wiley & Sons (1996).
3. E. Gamma, R. Helm, R. Johnson, J. Vlissides: *Design Patterns: Elements of Reusable Object-Oriented Software*. Reading, MA: Addison-Wesley (1995).
4. R. Harrison: *Symbian OS C++ for Mobile Phones*: New York: John Wiley and Sons (2003).
5. J. Noble, C. Weir: *Small Memory Software: Patterns for Systems with Limited Memory*: Addison Wesley (2000).
6. Sun Microsystem: J2ME Wireless Toolkit, available at: http://java.sun.com/products/j2mewtoolkit/ (last access April, 16, 2005), 2005
7. Wayfinder Systems: Wayfinder home page, available at: http://www.wayfinder.com (last access April, 16, 2005) (2005).

6
Pilot Projects

Fabio Bella, Filippo Forchino, Jarmo Kalaoja, Jürgen Münch, Alexis Ocampo, Mario Negro Ponzi, Marco Torchiano

Due to its newness, wireless Internet services engineering lacks explicit experience and quantitative data [1]. No historical data exists on related technologies, techniques and suitable software development process models. Some of the most critical consequences to be expected are unreliable project planning, incorrect effort estimates and high risk with respect to process, resource and technology planning. Under these circumstances, the quality of the target application turns out to be very hard to predict.

This chapter presents examples of wireless solutions engineered following the approach discussed in earlier chapters. Two pilot projects are examined from different perspectives such as engineering life cycle, technology and architecture. Special attention is given to the analysis of historical data gathered from the pilot projects [2, 3]. The chapter aims at providing managers and developers with a sense of the behaviour of projects in the wireless Internet domain by presenting the experience gathered through the development of pilot services within the context of the WISE (wireless internet service engineering) project.

The pilot services were developed following the iterative and incremental process described in Chapter 2 and both were over the same development periods. During each of the three iterations, the development focus was placed on a different set of requirements [4]. The first iteration took place during the period December 2001–December 2002 (13 months), the second iteration during the period February 2003–October 2003 (9 months) and the third iteration during the period November 2003–September 2004 (11 months). Figure 6.1 shows the time distribution of the three iterations.

The pilot projects represent significant examples of the application of the concepts described in other parts of the book. The approach followed to collect and analyse the data was based on the process modelling methodology introduced in Chapter 2 [5] and on goal-oriented measurement methods as discussed in [6]. Mutual relationships exist between this chapter and Chapter 3 'Technology', since technology issues represent one of the most important keys for understanding the behaviour of the projects under observation [7]. The terminology introduced in Chapter 4 'Architecture' is consequently adopted to show the high-level architecture of the pilot services.

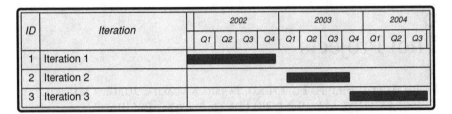

ID	Iteration	2002				2003				2004		
		Q1	Q2	Q3	Q4	Q1	Q2	Q3	Q4	Q1	Q2	Q3
1	Iteration 1											
2	Iteration 2											
3	Iteration 3											

FIGURE 6.1. Iteration overview.

Many of the results presented in this chapter are based on previous work published by the authors [8–11].

This chapter is organised around two main sections, one for each pilot project. Each section contains:

- a brief description of the pilot service,
- an overview of the process that has been applied to its development,
- a discussion of the historical data gathered during the development,
- a discussion of the main technologies applied and
- a description of the high-level architecture.

At the end of the chapter, a final section discussed major domain-specific issues observed during the development activities.

6.1 Pilot 1

Pilot service 1 provided a solution for real-time stock tracking on mobile devices, allowing the user to view real-time quotes across the whole market or else to define individual watch lists. The company responsible for this development is a provider of high-end trading services on the Internet, aimed at banks and brokers. The pilot was the adaptation of an existing web-based information service. Following pilot development, critical usability issues arose due to the huge amount of data needed by a financial operator to perform an analysis and the small size of the display on mobile devices. The end-user paid for Internet traffic to and from mobile devices with charging based on data volume and not on connection time. Since frequent refreshing of a large amount of financial data was required, the adoption of push technology instead of pull technology was an important issue, since it avoided unnecessary data refreshes for the user, thus reducing running costs.

6.1.1 Applied Process

Figure 6.2 shows the process used during each of the three iterations by the organisation in charge of Pilot 1's development. The process was the product of tailoring

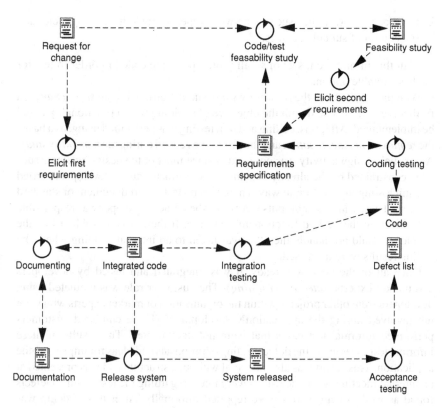

FIGURE 6.2. Overview process Pilot 1.

the reference process model presented in Chapter 2 of this book. The reference process model phases can be mapped to Pilot 1's process as follows:

- The *requirements phase* includes the activities *elicit first requirements*, *code/test feasibility study* and *elicit second requirements*.
- The *coding phase* consists only of the activity *coding testing*.
- The *testing phase* includes the activities *integration testing*, *documenting*, *release system* and *acceptance testing*.

Due to the fact that this organisation develops its code on top of an existing application, the name of the customer requirements document is *request for change*. This document was analysed in one meeting (elicit first requirements). This meeting had the purpose of establishing what could be implemented and what should be carried out as a feasibility study (*code/test feasibility study*). The feasibility study was carried out to look for answers to the following issues:

1. Select a set of mobile devices with the right display capabilities for presenting stock information. In this application it is important to avoid user scrolling of data. Push technology was found suitable for this kind of application.

2. Look at network issues such as network type, bandwidth, coverage, etc. and select a set of suitable devices.

With this information, sets of small prototypes were coded in order to test for the best suitable option.

With the results from the *feasibility study* and the original *request for change*, a further meeting was held with the objective of deciding which functionality could be implemented. After this, coding and unit testing was performed using, as a basis, the *requirements specification* and the prototypes coded during the *feasibility study*. An explicit design activity was not needed since most of the design related issues were constrained by the already existing server infrastructure. Developers carried out unit testing in an informal way. There was no test report document or standard where test cases, inputs or outputs were described. Each developer was responsible for delivering the desired functionality on time. If there was a problem that the developer could not handle then this was taken to an internal meeting where the testing results were discussed.

Once all of the code was ready, it was integrated and tested by developers and market experts (*integration testing*). The customer role was emulated using developers from other projects within the organisation or market experts who were not involved during the application's development. These emulated customers performed informal test cases that were not documented. The results of these informal test cases led to the defect finding or proposals and ideas for improving the application. This report was also informal without a structure and was presented at an internal meeting where decisions were made regarding the test results. Defects found as well as suggestions were reported informally. After this, a demo was packaged into the device and submitted to the market division for further tests including UI interaction. At the same time, developers were writing the technical and user manuals (*documentation*). For each of the different types of clients, the product had to be customised and packaged. A review by the market division approved releasing the system (*release system*), which was finally tested by friendly end-users for some time (*acceptance testing*) before its official final release.

6.1.2 Effort Baselines

For the analysis, the effort data related to the single activities were consolidated into the three main phases: *requirements, development* and *test* phase.

Over 750 man-days of effort were spent on the overall development of the service. Figure 6.3 shows the distribution between the three iterations. The greatest effort was spent during the first iteration (about 340 man-days in 13 months) and during this iteration, the existing server infrastructure had to be adapted to support the wireless version of the information service. The first version of the wireless service was implemented in WML and derived from an existing HTML version of the service provided over the traditional Internet. During the second iteration, a Java version of the service was created for Blackberry devices. The choice of a full programming language like Java was motivated by the need for push functionality which was not supported by WML and by the desire to explore Java's graphical

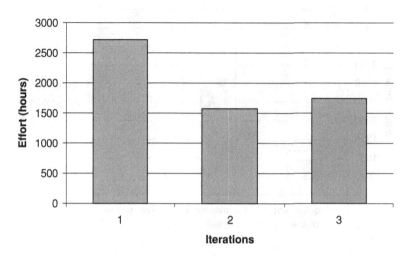

FIGURE 6.3. Effort distribution (broken down by iterations).

features. During the third iteration, the service developed in the second iteration containing Blackberry-specific libraries was modified to be able to run on devices with a colour display without the assistance of any proprietary library. The first attempts to run the service on UMTS devices in the Italian market had to be abandoned due to the difficulties encountered when trying to deploy the client application on the devices. In the first half of 2004, only one network provider was distributing UMTS devices in Italy and its policy was to protect them against the deployment of non-trusted applications. Regarding the effort spent on the last two iterations, the amount was comparable if we take into account that the second iteration was shorter than the third iteration (about 200 man-days in 9 months against about 220 man-days in 11 months).

Figure 6.4 shows the effort spent on the different phases during the whole project. During each iteration, most of the effort was spent on implementing the service (73% of the overall effort was in the development phase). Relatively little effort was spent during the requirements phase (20%). This was mainly due to two reasons, firstly, the functional requirements of the service were already known at the beginning of the project since the same functionality already provided by the existing web-based version of the service had to be provided on the wireless Internet and secondly, due to the novelty of the technologies applied and the many non-functional requirements, mainly concerned with usability and performance-related issues, could often not be clarified before coding commenced. During the second iteration, greater effort was spent on the requirements phase than in the first iteration (about 65 man-days). One of the main reasons was the introduction of time-consuming feasibility studies performed to explore the capabilities of Java-related technologies. This was deemed necessary when it was observed that during

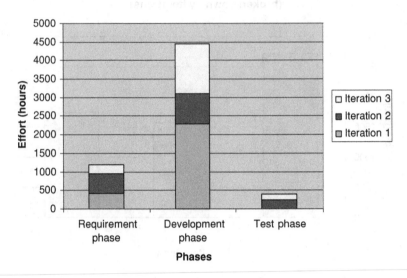

FIGURE 6.4. Effort overview.

the first iteration a great deal of the effort spent on coding did not produce any tangible result but was absorbed in exploring technology-related issues that could not be understood without resorting to code. Feasibility studies were introduced to explicitly gather this kind of experience and to understand better how the decision-making process concerned with the selection of requirements should be carried out. A total of about 65 man-days–over 8% of the overall development effort–was needed to perform the feasibility studies.

Concerning the test phase, the relatively low amount of effort spent on it, a total amount of about 50 man-days which was approximately 7% of the overall effort, can be explained by the low complexity of the functions required and the greater priority placed on exploring new technologies than on achieving a version of the service to be considered mature enough for the market. This priority led to the decision to skip the test phase at the end of the first iteration due to deadline pressure. On the other hand, it should also be borne in mind that some effort was spent by third-party organisations in evaluating the service and that this effort was not recorded since it did not happen within the scope of the WISE project. The organisations were interested in buying the client application and evaluated the business model underlying the service as well as the overall usability of the service.

6.1.3 Technology

The development of the pilot service began in the first iteration using a thin-client approach. Since the reference desktop client application is web-based, it was natural to try to adopt the same design choices on wireless clients. This was considered to be the best approach because of the limited service interaction and because of the much larger base of WML-enabled devices (see Chapter 3). However, after the first iteration, differences and incompatibilities between wireless clients and the technological limitations of the thin-client approach suggested a switch to a fat-client approach. In order to keep the installed client base large, the selected technology was Java2 Micro Edition (J2ME™), as was used in the second pilot. It was then necessary to build up a server-side adaptation layer (in order to push and pull data to and from the same server that works with desktop clients) to communicate with the new client. In the third iteration it was then possible to add full interaction, and the developed pilot is now a commercial product.

Technological constraints concerned with user interface (UI) classes[1] and a market analysis suggested targeting specific devices that contained proprietary J2ME extensions. While this approach restricts the application to a specific family of devices, it is easy to port the pilot service to different devices provided the non-standard libraries are ported, too. This was not seen as an overwhelming task. Compare this approach with the one adopted by Pilot 2, which developed in-house UI libraries (see later in this chapter).

For Pilot 1 network bandwidth and latency did not represent a critical issue. This was particularly true during the second and third iteration when the wireless data networks used were very reliable and stable and provided a data rate comparable with home dial-up wired Internet connections.

This pilot application demonstrated that the thin-client approach often turns out to be inapplicable. In practice, its use should be limited to providing data lists, which have a very limited interaction. As soon as graphical feedback and bi-directional interaction become more important together with problems with different screen sizes, the impossibility of precisely setting the position and size of pictures and limited interaction capability, force designers to switch to fat clients.

6.1.4 Architecture

During the first iteration a thin-client approach was adopted. This was changed for the second to a fat-client approach. The third iteration architecture should be considered as an enhanced version of this, which better supported bi-directional interaction between clients and server.

Figure 6.5 depicts the system architecture (structural viewpoint). The *Blackberry MDS Proxy Server* is the server responsible for enabling access to the service and is also responsible for formatting the data used by the wireless clients. It supports bi-directional interaction between subscribers and the server and interacts with the same subscription server accessed by wired clients. Client software is deployed on

---

[1] The J2ME standard does not provide any class for building complex tables. Because of the business-oriented origin of the Blackberry devices, the company had added some proprietary extensions to their J2ME implementation targeted at handling data.

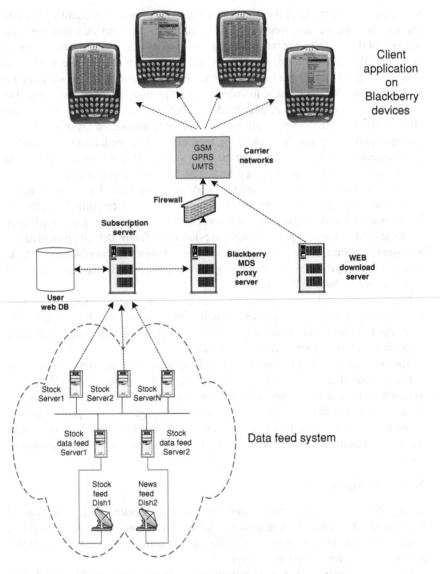

FIGURE 6.5. System architecture (structural viewpoint).

Blackberries as an application coded in J2ME. The *WEB Download Server* allows downloading of the application directly over the air.

The *User Web DB* is the same database as that accessed by the thin client developed during the first iteration. The database acts as a user management module that authenticates clients during the login phase.

The whole system is integrated with the pre-existing server environment called *Data Feed System*, which provides financial market variations (called

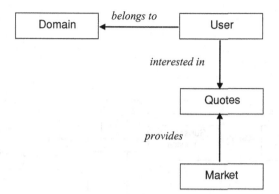

FIGURE 6.6. Domain information model.

ticks or *quotes*). Access to stock markets, orders, trades and updates of user accounts/positions are handled by the *trading system* (not shown in the figure).

The domain information model (Figure 6.6) shows the basic concepts used to model the application using common terms in the trading context.

Table 6.1 describes the elements of Figure 6.6.

The main driver in the design of the architecture for this pilot was to reuse as much as possible of the existing infrastructure already supporting a web-based service.

The functional structure of the pilot is presented in Figure 6.7, showing the typical *subdivision* into high-level domains as prescribed by the reference architecture and the services 'quotes' and 'news' that belong to the Investnet domain. Investnet is the back-end domain for the existing web-based application.

The responsibilities of the functional elements are presented in Table 6.2.

The deployment of the functional elements onto the network nodes is shown in Figure 6.8. The services 'quotes' and 'news' are located on a back-end node that provides the information for the whole system. The management services and the 'subscription' service are located on a server node shared with the web-based service.

The wireless-specific part of the service is located on a dedicated access node that communicates with the mobile device (where the end-user service is located)

TABLE 6.1. Trading information model description

Conceptual element	Description
User	It uses stock-exchange information from mobile device.
Domain	The domain defines the context for user identification, authentication, authorisation and accounting.
Quotes	The quotes represent the values of stocks that come from the markets.
Market	A market represents a real-world stock-exchange market that provides quote updates.

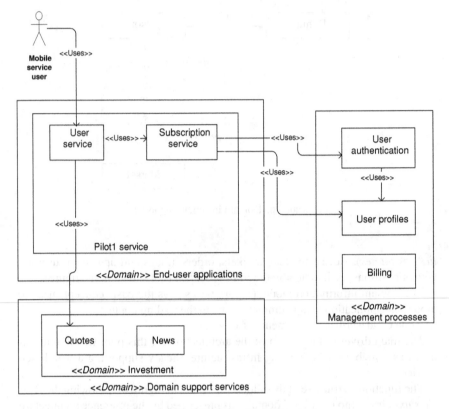

FIGURE 6.7. Pilot 1 functional structure.

through a data service. The data service is specific for the device chosen for the implementation.

6.2 Pilot 2

The second pilot service developed a multiplayer online game for mobile devices. It features real-time interaction amongst many players who share a virtual

TABLE 6.2. Responsibilities of functional elements

Conceptual element	Responsibility
User service	Provides mobile stock-exchange service for mobile users on a Blackberry device.
Subscription service	Manages the business logic of Pilot 1 service, i.e., enables client access and handles quotes information.
User authentication	Takes care of authentication, security and user classes.
Quotes service	Provides stock quote information.

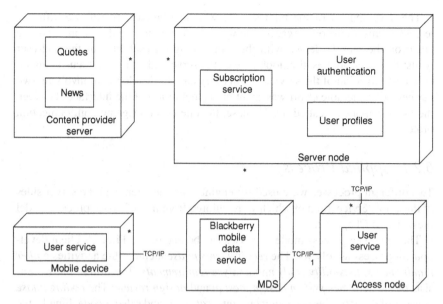

FIGURE 6.8. Deployment of Pilot 1.

environment consisting of a fantasy world map. Players can collect items and transport them to other locations, chat and fight against enemies and against each other. A player's character can also develop during the game as victories in battle or the completion of special missions award them experience points that can be used to upgrade attributes of speed, strength, dexterity, etc.

Games of this kind are popular in the wired Internet world where they are commonly called massively multiplayer online role playing games (MMORPG). Their success lies in the detailed implementation of a huge virtual world shared by many players (in the order of hundreds) who are given just adventure clues without a predefined path to follow. Being a role playing game, most of the fun and addictiveness lie in the development of a player's character by searching for or trading to get rare and powerful items for facing mighty opponents or just for collector's fever.

In the mobile world, this kind of game has not yet boomed, though there is an undeniable interest amongst network operators and gaming companies. Even if multiplayer games are considered by many to be the next step in wireless gaming, a massive release onto the market has been delayed for several reasons:

–technical limitations of the mobile terminals and the data network radio access;
–the huge amount of data exchange (due to real time interaction) combined with
   the relatively high cost of data traffic and
–the high cost of game maintenance, since such games require powerful servers
   able to guarantee a good quality of service 24/7 to many users.

The development of the pilot service was distributed between two different teams/organisations: one organisation was responsible for the development of the client on the mobile device with the focus being on usability for the end-user whilst the other organisation took care of the server side with the focus being on easy customisation of the service. As in every case of development involving two partners, considerable effort was spent on the definition of the interfaces between the two components called, in this case, the client–server game communication protocol.

6.2.1 Applied Process

Two different processes were used for engineering the client and the server sides of this pilot service, both of which were tailored from the reference process model presented in Chapter 2.

The reference process model's phases can be mapped to Pilot 2's client development process as follows: The *requirements phase* includes the activities *gather requirements, feasibility study* and *analyse requirements*. The *design phase* consists of the activities *system design, design* and *design review*. The *coding phase* consists of the activities *code, unit test, integrate code* and *release code*. Finally, the *testing phase* includes the activities *plan tests, build test framework, test system, test usability, acceptance test* and *analyse defect*.

The organisation in charge of client development followed the traditional software development life cycle phases (see Figure 6.9). However, there were activities that were performed specifically for the development of wireless Internet services.

The requirements were gathered as two types: request for change of existing services, or development from scratch of new services. This information was written in the *requests from customer* and usually demanded the use of innovative UI interaction. This is a challenge for any organisation, because there is little information on what type of libraries, COTS products or open source solutions are most appropriate for developing a user-friendly wireless Internet service. Research for the best options was performed in an activity called *analyse user interface feasibility requirements*. The idea was to validate the UI interaction requirements against the capabilities of existing libraries developed either internally or externally. Following this analysis, decisions were made to accept or reject UI requirements. Some of the requirement feasibilities were unclear and these were further analysed in another activity called *feasibility study*. This study was different from the previous because it covered other important aspects of wireless Internet services such as wireless networks, bandwidth, quality of service and security amongst others (see Chapter 1). Once all the technical issues were resolved, the requirements were specified in the *Software Requirements Specification*, passed to the *design phase*. The client-side service design was impacted by the characteristics of wireless Internet services. Optimisation was needed to improve the performance of the application, specifically for the game server.

The code was then produced, unit tested, integrated and released (*coding phase*). The client developers performed their unit tests using the 'J2ME Wireless Toolkit 2.1', a client emulator allowing the running of Midlets and emulating the

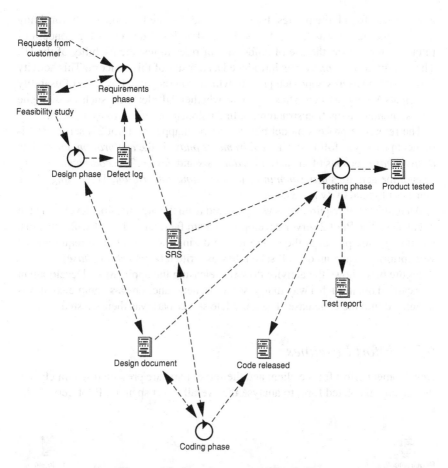

FIGURE 6.9. Overview process Pilot 2 client.

functionality of a mobile device. Specific components were tested on cellphones such as network modules since they were critical for the rest of the application. The graphic library components were tested separately before including them in the application. The client part contained four modules:

- the communication module,
- the game engine module,
- the interface module and
- the data storage module.

These were tested separately before integration. The set of communication components was called the 'transport layer' and to test this, a server emulator ('server stub') had to be developed. The interface module component integration tests were performed using the 'J2ME Wireless Toolkit 2.1'.

The complete functionality of the system (client and server) was tested using the real environment (*testing phase*). No emulators were used during these tests. If

144   F. Bella et al.

a defect was found, the parties discussed it and assigned responsibility for fixing it. Once the defect was fixed, it was declared a closed defect. A big concern of pilot developers was the use of guidelines or rules to test the usability of the UI. The activity *test usability* was introduced as a result of this concern. This activity is based on Nielsen's approach [12], in which experts guided by a set of usability principles known as heuristics evaluate whether UI elements such as dialogue boxes, menus, navigation structure, online help, etc. conform to user needs.

The reference process model phases can be mapped to Pilot 2's server development process as follows: The *requirements phase* is the *exploration phase*. The *design phase* consists of the activities *analysis* and *design*. The *coding phase* consists of the activities *programming* and *continuous integration*. The *testing phase* consists of the activity *test system*.

An initial set of requirements was gathered from the organisation developing the client side. The Pilot 2 server development team familiarised itself with the tools, technology and practices they were to use during the project. The requirements were prioritised and an overall schedule was written (*exploration phase*).

Figure 6.10 shows the activity flow for releasing the application. Development was carried out in such a way that as soon as a new function was completed, it was integrated into the code base. The complete server part was then retested.

6.2.2 Effort Baselines

Development effort for the client and the server parts are presented separately and then in an aggregated form to analyse the overall effort spent on Pilot Service 2.

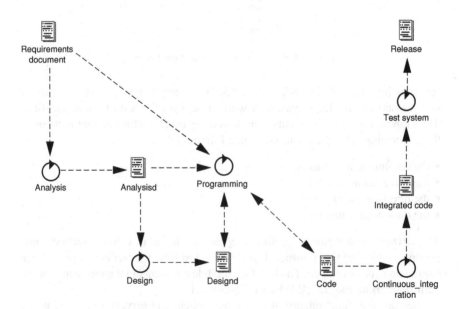

FIGURE 6.10. Overview process Pilot 2 server release phase.

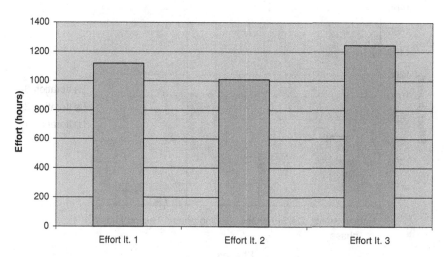

FIGURE 6.11. Effort distribution–client side (broken down by iterations).

About 420 man-days were needed to develop the client side of the pilot service. Figure 6.11 shows that a comparable amount of effort was spent during each of the three iterations. During the first iteration, about 140 man-days were spent over a 13-month period; in the second, about 125 man-days over 9 months and during the third iteration, about 150 man-days over 11 months.

Figure 6.12 shows the same effort data broken down by phases. During each iteration and therefore during the whole project, most of the effort was spent on coding (about 50% of the overall effort), whereas the design phase took the least effort (about 14%). The requirements and the testing phase required a comparable amount of effort (the requirements phase took 80 man-days, 19% of effort, the test phase 70 man-days, 17%).

Looking more closely at these figures, it should be noted that most of the requirements were specified and prioritised during the first iteration. After that, at the beginning of each iteration, the parties involved agreed a new set of requirements to be addressed and further specification was done verbally and by email. The greater effort spent on the requirements phase during the second and the third iterations can be explained by the introduction of feasibility studies commencing with the second iteration. This was needed since, in a similar manner to Pilot 1, it became clear after the first iteration that many technology-related issues could only be clarified through coding. A total of about 30 man-days (i.e., over 7% of the effort spent on the development of the client side) were needed for feasibility studies.

Concerning the design phase, less effort was spent on design in succeeding iterations, explained by the fact that many of the most relevant design-related decisions had already been made. Although design-related activities were performed during the last iteration in order to address design issues concerned with the

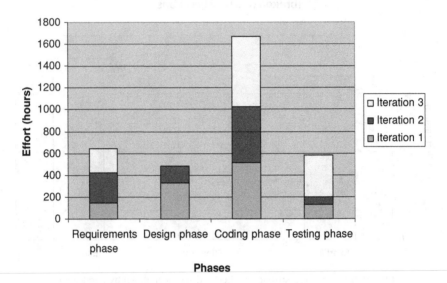

FIGURE 6.12. Effort distribution–client side (broken down by phases).

communication between client and server side, this did not lead to any change in the main design document and the negligible resulting effort was not collected as design-related but as coding-related, since the problems were informally addressed through verbal communication and immediately solved through changes in code.

The coding phase was carried out in a systematic way based on the prioritised requirements and included automated unit testing. A comparable amount of effort was spent on this phase during each iteration of between 60 and 80 man-days per iteration.

About 17% of the effort was spent on the system test phase with the bulk carried out at the end of the third iteration when the whole system was ready. Deadline pressure and the high priority placed on the exploration of available technologies were additional reasons for shifting the main test activities to the end of the project. Another important reason was the intrinsic difficulty of testing applications on mobile devices. The project was torn between the two extremes of either testing on real devices which was extremely time-consuming due to the lack of automation or using emulators, which were not reliable substitutes for real devices. As an inevitable consequence, the testing process turned out to be difficult to estimate and to plan. The situation was made even worse if the application had to run and therefore had to be tested on different devices.

The server-side development took about 260 man-days. Two different organisations were involved in the development, the organisation first responsible for the server left the project after the end of the first iteration and therefore another partner assumed the role for the remaining two iterations. Figure 6.13

Effort distribution – Pilot 2 (server side)
(broken down by iterations)

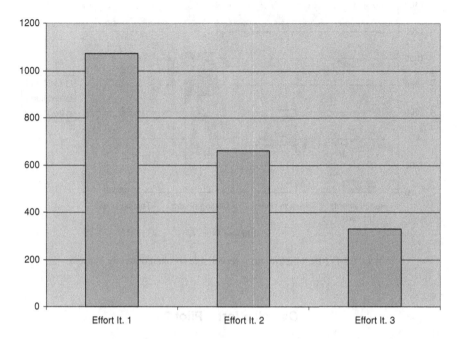

FIGURE 6.13. Effort distribution–server side (broken down by iterations).

shows that most of the effort related to the server side was spent during the first iteration (135 man-days, 52% of effort). At the end of the first iteration, the basic infrastructure, an Enterprise Java Beans server, had been set. The same infrastructure was deployed during the second iteration on servers hosted by the other partner and enhanced during the two iterations to support all requirements formalised at the beginning of the first iteration.

Figure 6.14 shows the distribution of the effort spent on the server side in the three development phases. Since the whole development was driven by the organisation responsible for the client side, very little effort was spent on the requirements and on the testing phase (about 10 man-days, 4% of effort, each phase). Similar to the client-side development, there was again less effort spent on design in the last two iterations. The main effort was spent on coding-related activities (160 man-days, 62% of effort).

A similar picture is shown in Figure 6.15 where the organisational involvement becomes clearer and although the whole development was driven by the organisation responsible for the client side, comparable efforts were needed to address design-related issues and to implement the service.

To achieve Pilot Service 2, a total of about 680 man-days were required. Figure 6.16 shows the distribution of the overall effort among the four main phases.

Overall effort – Pilot 2 (server side)

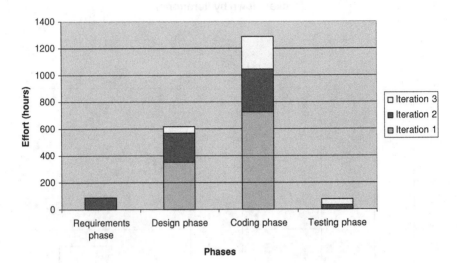

FIGURE 6.14. Effort distribution–server side (broken down by phases).

Overall effort – Pilot 2

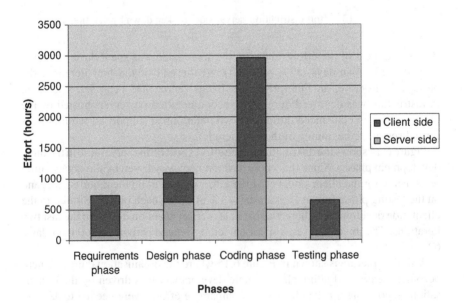

FIGURE 6.15. Overview organisations' involvement.

Effort distribution – Pilot 2

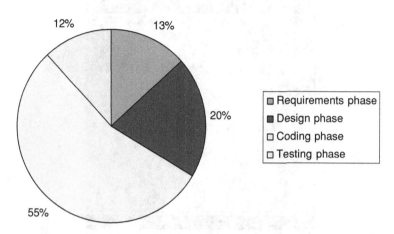

FIGURE 6.16. Effort distribution–Pilot 2 (broken down by phases).

As usual, most of the effort was spent on coding (55%), design-related activities required about 20% of the work whereas the requirements and the test phases together took up the remaining 25%.

6.2.3 Technology

The features of the service are such that the choice of a fat-client approach is practically mandatory. The game needs a complex UI with many different screens that must react to user actions. The main game screen, for example, shows a player-controlled character moving on a map together with monsters or other players' characters. Players must be allowed to easily carry out a multitude of actions ranging from chatting to fighting, from browsing their inventory to checking out the game hall of fame.

Use of a fat client also allows multimedia effects such as sound effects, music and animated and full-screen graphics since the application has full control of the device display.

The service is organised as a traditional client/server application where multiple clients running on mobile devices connect to a multi-threaded server listening for connections on the Internet. Mobile devices may connect to the Internet in one of several ways including GPRS, UMTS, Wi-Fi, etc. but this is absolutely transparent to the two parties since they both simply rely on a TCP/IP connection. They communicate through a custom binary communication protocol that has been designed to be simple and minimal.

On the client side, J2ME has been selected as the development language, a choice driven mainly by the fact that it is a widely supported standard. Though manu-facturers distribute their own proprietary extensions to J2ME, only the standard

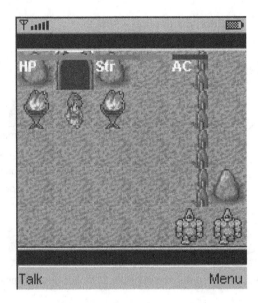

FIGURE 6.17. Sample screenshot of Pilot Service 2.

APIs were used in this project in order to ensure maximum portability of the code. The lack of 'nice', game-oriented UI libraries made it necessary to develop a lightweight, extendable GUI library. This library was then used to create the dialogues of the client application.

The target devices are mainly mobile phones, characterised by a relatively small display backed by limited processing and multimedia capabilities. The UI treats screen width and height as variables, rearranging the display of text and graphics dynamically.

The target devices' multimedia capabilities usually include:

– MP3/Wave sound support (for sound effects or sampled music),
– MIDI music support (for FM music),
– PNG is the only supported graphic format (J2ME standard, on MIDP 2 JPEG can also be supported) and
– vibration and potentially also embedded camera.

On the server side, the natural choice was to use a similar Java technology: Java 2 Enterprise Edition (J2EE). This allowed some common code to be shared between client and server or to be reused, i.e., the communication protocol library. The server is integrated with an external service management component, used to perform common tasks like authentication and service subscription.

6.2.4 Architecture

The networked environment (structural viewpoint) for the game (shown in Figure 6.18) is described next. Clients had access to a GPRS or UMTS network connected

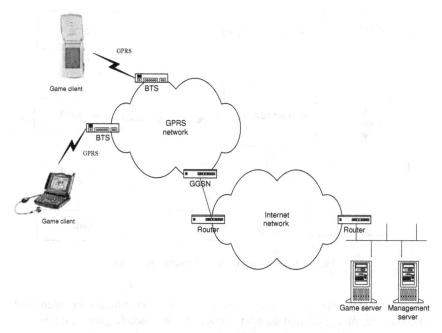

FIGURE 6.18. System architecture (structural viewpoint).

to the Internet. Having this access to the Internet, clients were able to connect to the Game Server. The Game Server made use of a series of Management Services (such as authentication and authorisation), which were provided by other servers. The system context affects the software architecture mainly as a rationale for the structuring of architecture and defines the nodes used in deployment views.

Figure 6.19 shows the domain information model for the game. The model defines the terms of the domain and is important for the design of data shared in architectural interfaces.

The objects presented in the figure are described in more detail in Table 6.3.

One of the main goals achieved was to identify the generic application domain services that are common for different kinds of computer games (and possibly other entertainment services). These generic services can be reused as a platform for different game applications. The game conceptual model from the first iteration is shown in Figure 6.20. The architectural model also shows the main technology choices on both the client and the server sides. An opportunity for using a previously developed generic transport service was also identified. In architecture modelling at the conceptual level, the emphasis was on understanding the relation between the game client and the server and the services available from the service management domain of the reference architecture.

The corresponding conceptual deployment model of these services and its behavioural view are presented in the notation examples within the Architecture chapter. Later iterations of the game architecture added services needed by two

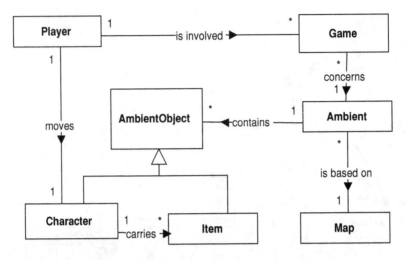

FIGURE 6.19. Game domain information model.

new stakeholders who were a game designer and a game manager and identified potential generic application support services for the mobile gaming domain of the reference architecture (Figure 6.21).

The objects presented in the figure are described in more detail in Table 6.4.

TABLE 6.3. Game information model description

Object	Description
Player	A Player represents a user of the game service. An instance of this class is created when the user subscribes to the service and it is removed when the user unsubscribes from the service.
Game	A Game represents the fact that a player is playing the game in a specific Ambient (op cit). For each Ambient only one game could exist for a player. An instance of this class is created when a user requests a new game and it is destroyed when the game ends. A game ends when the Character the player uses in the game is dead. A game can be suspended and later resumed.
Ambient	An Ambient is an environment where a set of users each play their own game moving their own character. An Ambient consists of: −a map, −a set of items placed in the environment described by the map and −a set of characters acting in the environment described by the map.
Map	A map is the static description of an Ambient. It is the landscape where the game takes place, e.g., a castle, a forest, a dungeon, etc.
AmbientObject	An AmbientObject is an object that is contained in an Ambient. Both Character and Item are sub-classes of AmbientObject.
Character	A Character is an entity controlled by a player, moving and acting in an Ambient. An instance of this class is created when the player requests a new character and it is destroyed when the character dies.
Item	An Item is an object (e.g., a treasure, a weapon, a spell book, etc.) that is present in the Ambient. An object could be carried by a character.

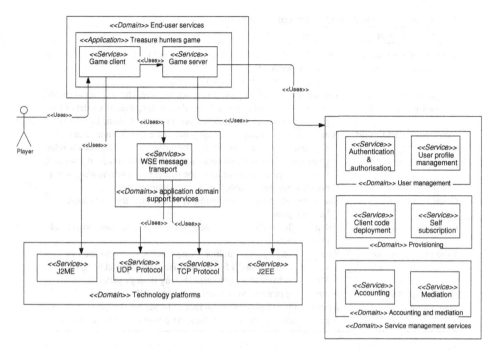

FIGURE 6.20. Game conceptual structural model.

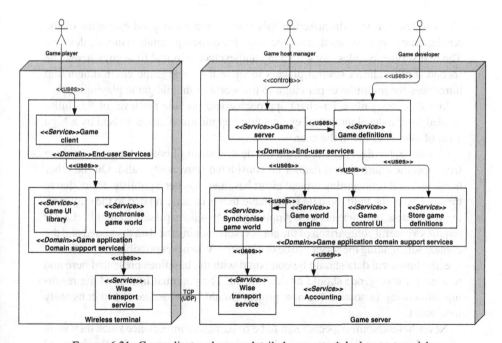

FIGURE 6.21. Game client and server detailed conceptual deployment model.

TABLE 6.4. Conceptual model element descriptions

Conceptual element	Description
The game client (i.e., Player game world)	The game status of region of game world as visible to a single player in wireless terminal.
Game UI library	A gaming-oriented lightweight GUI library.
The game server (i.e., Server game world)	The status of the whole game world at the server. The information model of the game world is based on the domain information model of the game. Provides a GUI to control and monitor the game in progress.
Synchronise game world	Handles session management and synchronisation of game status between player game worlds and the server game world via a wireless connection. This is based on an application level messaging protocol that exchanges domain information model based information, using broadcasting and a publish–subscribe design pattern.
Game definitions	The game definitions (maps, items, monsters, etc.) for the treasure hunter's game.
Game world engine	Calculates the results of player actions for player, the game world and other players.
Store game definitions	Stores adventure game definitions (maps, items, monsters, etc.) in various formats (ASCII file formats like XML, Java classes, etc.). Monster behaviour is implemented using strategy patterns.
Wise transport service	A messaging protocol via a wireless TCP or UDP connection.
Accounting	Authentication of players and storage of player profile information. A proxy service is provided by the service management component.

6.3 Conclusion

The wireless services discussed in this chapter represent good examples of the revolutionary applications that will be available on new generation mobile devices. The first service enables stock tracking and exchange in real time anywhere. The second service allows several players to share the same game environment and introduces the multiplayer paradigm to the world of mobile game playing.

In both cases, only a fat-client approach could provide the level of flexibility needed for the development of eye-catching applications characterised by a high level of interaction with the user.

Of course, the data gathered from the development of both pilot services came from specific contexts and cannot be considered universally valid. On the other hand, little data concerning typical effort baselines has been published and, due to the novelty of the field, no data is available that is directly related to the engineering of wireless Internet services. Applying the baselines presented in this chapter requires a careful comparison of the context surrounding the data discussed and the context surrounding the service to be engineered. Whenever possible, organisation-specific historical data should be compared with the baselines presented here and reasons for divergence should be determined. The potential impact of the resulting influencing factors on the new project should be investigated and constantly monitored.

Nevertheless, some aspects seem to be of particular importance since they were observed in both pilot projects and regarded in a similar way by the involved parties. In all cases observed, less effort was spent on design than on coding and most of the effort was spent on coding-related activities. This fact was regarded to be a consequence of the uncertainty inherent in this kind of project and the many unexpected issues that could be discovered only during coding. Feasibility studies took up to 8% of the overall effort and this data should be considered an underestimation of the real project behaviour, since during the first iteration the effort spent on feasibility studies was classified as coding. Our experience showed that feasibility studies represent a valid means for investigating requirements and documenting related decisions in the case of the wireless Internet. The percentage of effort spent on testing (between 7 and 12% of the overall effort) would probably turn out to be too low in the case of a mature service to be considered market ready. Testing turned out to be the most difficult phase to estimate and plan due to extremely time-consuming testing on real devices and the unreliability of emulators.

In general, the choice of an iterative and incremental life cycle was considered the only one possible in a field governed by uncertainty. Explicit process modelling together with data collection performed in accordance with the resulting process descriptions represented a viable and fruitful way for gathering high-quality lessons learned, since the facts analysed during post-mortem sessions were based on measurable evidence. This helped to get a well-founded understanding of project behaviour.

References

1. Basili, V.R.: Quantitative evaluation of software engineering methodology. *Proceedings of the First Pan-Pacific Computer Conference*, Melbourne, Australia (1985).
2. Basili, V.R., Caldiera, G., Rombach, H.D.: Experience factory. In: Marciniak, J.J. (ed.), *Encyclopaedia of Software Engineering*, Vol. 1, New York: John Wiley & Sons, 511–519: Ill., Lit. (2002).
3. Becker-Kornstaedt, U., Boggio, D., Muench, J., Ocampo, A., Palladino, G.: Empirically driven design of software development processes for wireless Internet services. In: O. Markku (ed.) et al.: *4th International Conference on Product-Focused Software Processes Improvement Profes 2002—Proceedings*. Berlin: Springer-Verlag, pp. 351–366:111. Lit (Lecture Notes in Computer Science 2559).
4. Boehm, B.W.: A spiral model for software development and enhancement. *IEEE Computer*, Vol. 21, no 5, pp. 61–72 (1988).
5. Becker-Kornstaedt, U., Hamann, D., Kempkens, R., Rösch, P., Verlage, M., Webby, R., Zettel, J.: Support for the process engineer: The spearmint approach to software process definition and process guidance. *Proceedings of the Eleventh Conference on Advanced Information Systems Engineering (CAISE '99)*, Lecture Notes in Computer Science, Springer-Verlag, Berlin, Heidelberg, New York (1999).
6. Solingen, R., Berghout, E.: *The Goal/Question/Metric Method: A Practical Guide for Quality Improvement of Software Development*, London: McGraw-Hill (1999).
7. Kerth, N.L.: *Project Retrospectives: A Handbook for Team Reviews*, New York: Dorset House Publishing (2001).

8. Bella, F., Münch, J., Ocampo, A.: Baselining wireless Internet service development—An experience report. In: Brito e Abreu, Fernando (ed.): *Proccedings of the Fifth Conference for Quality in Information and Communications Technology, QUATIC 2004*, Instituto Portugês da Qualidade, Porto, pp. 161–169: Ill., Lit. (2004).

9. Bella, F., Münch, J., Ocampo, A.: Capturing evidence from wireless Internet services development. In: O'Brien, Liam (ed.): *Proceedings of the EleventhInternational Workshop on Software Technology and Engineering Practice, STEP'2003*, IEEE Computer Society, Los Alamitos, pp. 33–39: Ill., Lit. (2004).

10. Bella, F., Münch, J., Ocampo, A.: Observation-based development of software process baselines: An experience report. *Arbeitskreis Software-Qualität Franken e.V.:CONQUEST 2004. Proccedings of the Eighth Conference on Quality Engineering in Software Technology*, Erlangen, pp. 31–43: Ill., Lit. (2004).

11. Ocampo A., Boggio, D., Münch J. and Palladino G.: Toward a reference process for developing wireless Internet services. *IEEE Transactions on Software Engineering*, Vol. 29, no. 12, pp. 1122–1134: Ill., Lit. (2003).

12. Nielsen J. and Mack R.L. (1994). *Usability Inspection Methods*, John Wiley & Sons.

7
Glossary

This chapter presents some project terminology definitions and a list of acronyms.

7.1 Terminology

Service
provision of function (e.g. game or user authentication). A service may be (possibly) implemented by one or more (software) products or components.

End user service
provides a function to the end user, usually via a mobile device. Examples: voice call, SMS, MMS, travel information, game, trading. Typically the end-user pays for service because the user recognises the value added.

Enabler service
provides a function that is used internally to implement an end user service. Examples: authentication, authorisation, billing, roaming, etc.

Application
software based system that implements one or more services. Typically it requires client part (on mobile device) and server part.

Component or module
part of application, considered from physical or logical point of view. Components in an application are described by UML component view.

7.2 Acronyms

A-GPS	Assisted GPS
ANSI	American National Standard Institute
API	Application Programming Interface
ARM	Advanced RISC Machines
ATL	Active Template Library
AWT	Abstract Window Library

Bluetooth	Wireless network standard. The name comes from Harald Blåtand, King of Denmark from approximately A.D. 940 to 985, and is used because of the Scandinavian origin of the original standard. Now formally standardised by the IEEE as 802.15.1
BREW	Binary Runtime Environment for the Wireless
CDC	Connected Device Configuration
CDMA	Code Division Multiple Access
CDMA/2000	Code Division Multiple Access (US 3rd generation technology)
cHTML	Compact HTML
CLDC	Connected Limited Device Configuration
COM	Component Object Model
CVM	CDC VM
DLL	Dynamic Link Library
DoJa	J2ME DoCoMo proprietary API specification over CLDC
DSA	Digital Signature Algorithm
DTD	Document Type Definition
ECDSA	Elliptic Curve DSA
EDGE	Enhanced Data for GSM Evolution/Enhanced Data for Global Evolution
Foma	Freedom of Mobile Multimedia Access
GPRS	General Packet Radio Service
GPS	Global Positioning System
GSM	Global System for Mobile communications
HTML	HyperText Markup Language
HTTP	HyperText Transfer Protocol
IDE	Integrated Development Environment
IEEE	Institute of Electrical and Electronic Engineers
IP	Internet Protocol
IR	InfraRed
ISDN	Integrated Services Digital Network
J2EE	Java 2 Enterprise Edition
J2ME	Java 2 Micro Edition
JSP	Java Server Page
J2SE	Java 2 Standard Edition
JAD	Java Application Descriptor
JNI	Java Native Interface
JPEG	Joint Photographic Expert Group
KVM	Kilobyte VM
LAN	Local Area Network
MAC	Machine Address Code/Medium Access Control
MFC	Microsoft Foundation Classes
MIDlet	MIDP-based application
MIDP	Mobile Information Device Profile
MVC	Model View Controller

NTT DoCoMo	Nippon Telephone and Telegraph (docomo means 'anywhere' in Japanese)
OBEX	OBjects EXchange
OS	Operating System
PDA	Personal Digital Assistant
RAM	Random Access Memory
RISC	Reduced Instruction Set Computer
SIG	Special Interest Group
SSL	Secure Sockets Layer
TCP	Transmission Control Protocol
TI	Texas Instruments
TLS	Transport Layer Security
UDP	Universal Datagram Protocol
UMTS	Universal Mobile Telecommunication System
URL/URI	Universal Resource Locator/Identifier
VM	Virtual Machine
WAN	Wide Area Network
WAP	Wireless Access Protocol
WCDMA	Wideband CDMA
WEP	Wireless Equivalent Privacy
Wi-Fi	Wireless Fidelity
WML	Wireless Markup Language
xDSL	X Digital Subscriber Line (x means of any type, usually A for Asymmetric or H for High-bitrate)
Xlet	Java Personal Profile Application Model
XML	eXtensible Markup Language
SDK	Software Development Kit
RPC	Remote Procedure Call

Index

(ANSI) C, 57
.NET (Compact Framework), 65, 67, 85

adaptation (of content, of application), 15, 18, 112, 132, 137
agile development (see also extreme programming), 28
alternative (optional) process, 10, 16, 29
Appforge Crossfire, 67
ARM, 42, 63, 68

bandwidth, 2, 17, 24, 35, 37, 120, 126, 137
Blackberry, 138, 140, 141
Bluetooth, 35, 41, 85, 127, 128
BREW, 45, 55, 108

C++, 43, 58, 63, 92, 107, 108, 120
C++/COM, 65
CDC, 49, 54
CDMA, 38, 55
cHTML, 22, 45, 47, 48, 107
CLDC, 49, 50, 54, 63, 92
client server, 116, 149
    client server—fat client, 33, 44, 68, 101, 102, 107, 108, 137, 149
    client server—thin client, 6, 33, 44, 49, 102, 108, 111, 136, 137, 138
cross-platform, 67, 108

deployment, 124, 15, 52, 71, 75, 82, 83, 124, 141, 153
device
    device computing power, 125
    device independence, 14, 18

device input, 122
device memory, 125
DoJa, 53

EDGE, 38
effort (baselines), 134, 144
emulation, 23, 104, 129
extreme programming (see also agile development), 14, 21, 104

feasibility study, 12, 16, 29, 101, 106, 122, 127, 133, 142, 145, 155

GPRS, 34, 38, 65, 72, 127, 138, 149
GPS/A-GPS, 43, 80, 128
GSM, 37

HTML, 20, 118, 134
HTTP, 45, 51, 76, 85, 91, 96, 113

iMode, 45, 47, 108
incremental development model, 11, 27, 103, 106, 131, 155
Intel StrongARM/XScale, 42
IR/infrared/IRDA, 35, 63
ISDN, 37
iterative process model, 11, 28, 131, 155

Java
    Java J2EE, 78, 86, 93, 115, 118, 150
    Java J2ME, 21, 43, 49, 55, 63, 67, 78, 86, 95, 96, 105, 108, 129, 137, 143, 149
    Java J2SE, 49, 51
    Java Javascript, 45

Java *(cont.)*
    Java JVM, 49
    Java KVM, 49, 51

latency, 24, 35, 38, 125, 137

MFC, 65, 123
Midlet, 21, 52
MIDP, 19, 51, 52, 55, 63, 86, 92,
    150
MIME, 46
Mophun, 67

OBEX, 35

Palm (OS), 41, 42, 43, 63, 67
PAN, 35
pattern, 17, 70, 77, 85, 87, 90, 100
pattern MVC/Model View Controller, 59,
    94, 95, 96, 97, 108, 122, 123, 124
PDA, PDA phone, 40, 41, 42, 66, 120
pearl system, 101
peer to peer, 112
Personal (Basis) Profile, 54, 63
piconets, 36
pilot projects, 11, 12, 19, 23, 71, 104, 121,
    126
PocketPC, 41, 65, 67
presentation (see also user interface), 109,
    17, 26
process model, 131

quality of service, 2, 16, 90, 141

reference process model, 133, 142, 144
RS232, 35

Sandbox, 40, 43, 67
SavaJe, 43

scalability, 16, 18, 28, 115, 116, 118
seamless mobile service, 18
security, 127, 22, 36
simulation, 23
Smartphone, 65
Spearmint, 10
spiral model, 28
Symbian/EPOC, 41, 42, 58
Symbian C++, 58

tablet PC, 40, 44
test framework, 12, 22, 104, 142
throwaway prototype model, 27
tier, 91, 114

UMTS, 34, 37, 39, 47, 135, 149
usability, 2, 12, 14, 17, 22, 25, 27, 80, 132,
    142, 144
user interface, GUI (see also presentation),
    16, 18, 25, 60, 77, 82, 92, 103, 108,
    120, 123, 137

Visual Basic, 65, 66, 67

WAN, 45
WAP, 19, 21, 22, 27, 45, 46, 47, 79, 105,
    108
W-CDMA, 39
Wi-Fi, 37, 42, 63, 65, 149
Windows CE/Windows Mobile, 41, 65
wireless characteristics, 29
WISE project, 11, 17, 23, 97
WML, 20, 40, 45, 47, 106, 107, 110, 112,
    120, 134, 137
WMLScript, 45

xDSL, 37
Xlet, 54, 55
XML, 17, 45, 65, 79, 106